Busy Mom SCD Cookbook
with Honey Sweetened Recipes

2008 Update with More Recipes and Resources

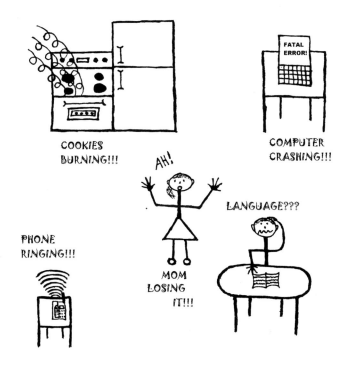

COOKIES
BURNING!!!

COMPUTER
CRASHING!!!

AH!

PHONE
RINGING!!!

MOM
LOSING
IT!!!

LANGUAGE???

By Tina Wade
GFCF
Wheat Free, Gluten Free, and Yeast Free
A US/UK FRIENDLY COOKBOOK
WITH AUTISM RESOURCES

Trafford
PUBLISHING

Order this book online at www.trafford.com/06-0110
or email orders@trafford.com

Most Trafford titles are also available at major online book retailers.

Edited by: E. Wade

Note for Librarians: A cataloguing record for this book is available from Library
and Archives Canada at www.collectionscanada.ca/amicus/index-e.html

Printed in Victoria, BC, Canada.

ISBN: 978-1-4120-8355-3

*We at Trafford believe that it is the responsibility of us all, as both individuals
and corporations, to make choices that are environmentally and socially sound.
You, in turn, are supporting this responsible conduct each time you purchase a
Trafford book, or make use of our publishing services. To find out how you are
helping, please visit www.trafford.com/responsiblepublishing.html*

*Our mission is to efficiently provide the world's finest, most comprehensive
book publishing service, enabling every author to experience success.
To find out how to publish your book, your way, and have it available
worldwide, visit us online at www.trafford.com/10510*

 www.trafford.com

North America & international
toll-free: 1 888 232 4444 (USA & Canada)
phone: 250 383 6864 ♦ fax: 250 383 6804 ♦ email: info@trafford.com

The United Kingdom & Europe
phone: +44 (0)1865 722 113 ♦ local rate: 0845 230 9601
facsimile: +44 (0)1865 722 868 ♦ email: info.uk@trafford.com

10 9 8 7 6 5

NOTE

THIS BOOK CONTAINS autism information and recipes for both GFCF and SCD diets. It is a record of the authors' experience with their child. As such, it should not be used as a diagnostic tool or as a guide in the treatment of any disorder. The diagnosis of any malady, use of nutritional supplements and implementation of special diets should be performed by a qualified physician/ nutritionist. The authors assume no responsibility or liability for the use or misuse of information contained herein.

DEDICATION

Thank you to my loving husband.
For helping his
computer illiterate and technology challenged wife
write this. Without his help
this definitely would not have been a possibility at all.

Love, Tina

Thank you to Chef Jeff Martin—American Orient Express,
for the big clue on honeys
having different water contents. It hadn't occurred to me.
It works great now!

Thank you to Brenda Davis—The Applecrate,
for getting Matthew and me
the extra food items not normally carried in the store
while Earl was gone to Iraq.

TABLE OF CONTENTS

THE
SPECIFIC
CARBOHYDRATE
DIET

INTRODUCTION

MY WIFE AND I have a 12-year old boy, Matthew. Matthew has High Functioning Autism. Over the past seven years, we have focused on modifying Matthew's diet and had some measure of success. We started out with the Gluten Free, Casein Free Diet in 2001. Shortly after starting GFCF, we decided to make it an all-natural diet as well, since we were constantly shopping in health food stores anyway. In 2005, we decided to do Dr. Gottschalk's Specific Carbohydrate Diet in conjunction with the GFCF diet. We spent one year with both diets (1 January 2005 to 31 December 2005), as planned, and returned to a GFCF-only diet. In 2006, we wrote the original version of this book to aid in preparing GFCF and SCD foods, and added some recipes in 2008.

This book contains recipes for the Gluten-Free Casein-Free Diet and the Specific Carbohydrate Diet. It also has recipes acceptable to both diets.

The Specific Carbohydrate Diet has indeed been a struggle. My family was successful at this only because of my wife's superior talent in the kitchen and our unwitting preparation through the Gluten and Casein Free Diet. Since we were already limited by our GFCF diet and had grown accustomed to some measure of deprivation, we were in training so to speak, for the more rigorous and severe SCD. It is important to note; Our success with these diets may have been aided by the fact that we had gone yeast-free and had done the PCA-Rx heavy-metal cleansing regimen prior to embarking upon our SCD adventure. In addition, we take an all or nothing approach; The entire family eats the same foods and takes the same supplements, not just Matthew (our autistic son).

While Matthew didn't exhibit the symptoms described by Elaine Gottschalk, our reading led us to believe bacterial overgrowth and consequently a weakened intestinal lining as described by Ms. Gottschalk might have been an underlying cause in his autism. Given this and the diet's innocuous menu, we proceeded with a one-year test of the SCD plan. There seems to be something to the theory of indigestible disaccharides leading to intestinal overpopulation of less-desirable-bacteria, but we have no solid evidence to present.

The SCD diet is hard, make no mistake. While on the diet, I often looked back on the "good old days" of GFCF when we were free. We have not seen a dramatic improvement like we had with some of our other treatments (e.g. magnesium and B6 described below). Nor have we seen the marked improvement that accompanied our use of the GFCF diet and other supplements. I think we did not expect much visible improvement. What we were looking for, however, was the internal intestinal healing, the main goal of the SCD diet, to improve his overall condition. Once we achieved 12 months on the SCD, we reverted back to a GFCF-only diet. GFCF on its own is a cake walk compared to GFCF combined with SCD. The two together are so limiting, there is almost nothing left to eat. At least it seems that way sometimes.

Vitamins and Supplements

(Evaluated by a nutritionist, of course)

We also included a host of vitamins and other supplements in our diet. The list built up over the years, but I believe the most significant impact came from the addition of B6 and magnesium.

After a while on the GFCF diet Matthew's condition had improved significantly, but he rarely spoke. When he did speak, his vocabulary was extreme limited and he seemed unable to express an idea autonomously. His conversations consisted mainly of movie scripts recited from memory. We came across some research on B6/ magnesium and autism by Dr. Bernard Rimland; we decided to try it.

The results were startling: The next day, while picking up Matthew at his elementary school, his Second Grade teacher Mrs. Ford mentioned she had to scold him for talking out-of-turn. While this is common among second-graders, Matthew never spoke without prompting from the teacher and she initially could not find the small, offending talker. Her difficulty was compounded because she knew Matthew never spoke. After several instances of being unable to locate the little talker disrupting her lecture, she realized it was Matthew. She was very excited as she reported this to us at the end of the day. This was a special milestone in our autism adventure.

After completing our experiment with SCD, we decided to add dietary enzymes to our normal GFCF diet. Since we were already getting our vitamins from Kirkman's, we initially went with their Enzym-Complete/DPP-IV®; it seems to cover all the food groups and we've eliminated some minor digestion problems. Now, we're trying Peptidase Complete (also from Kirkman); it seems to be targeted more toward our gluten/casein issue. We have not, however, adopted the use of digestive enzymes to allow Matthew to consume gluten and casein-foods.

In 2006, we added L-carnosine and zinc as supplements to the diet. We based this addition on a study of the effect of this amino acid on autism patients. Since it appeared to help the participants in speech and social interaction, and L-carnosine already occurs naturally in muscle tissue, we added it to our regimen. Once again, this dietary addition was reviewed by a nutritionist and all three family-members take the supplement.

OTHER TREATMENTS

As I SAID, we can't attribute all our advances and success to disciplined adherence to diets. While we feel the diets play a central role, we also had numerous instance of startling improvements brought on by unlikely treatments.

The Sissel Sit-Fit cushion and "In Your Pocket's" weighted vest are options tried on the basis of having no downside and being completely innocuous, (i.e. unlikely to cause any harm). In the worst-case scenario, such things simply wouldn't work-they would have no effect. Much to our surprise, the weighted vest seemed to have a calming effect which allowed Matthew to tune-out distractions and focus in a classroom environment. The sit-fit cushion somehow complimented and reinforced this effect. Generally, use of the vest improved his performance by one letter grade (sometimes he would forget to put it back on). Since the cushion was always in his seat, we have no with and without comparison for it. These cushions and weighted vests were recommended to us by an occupational therapist. The weighted vest involves specific weights and times; the schedule should be developed by a therapist. By the time he was 10 years old, the weighted vest and cushion were no longer needed.

We have also tried other very non-invasive therapies like chiropractic adjustment, audio integration therapy, and sauna. Since these therapies don't seem to introduce internal biological variables, I see them as very low risk (I have a "what-the-heck" category of treatments).

We also investigated non-stick surfaces on cookware. We were concerned over the possibility of compounds (particularly non-organic) from the non-stick surfaces transferring to Matthew's food. Unable to find what I considered to be worthwhile data and not willing to expend a great deal of time on the search, we opted for iron cookware. Lodge Logic makes iron cookware seasoned with vegetable oils for a natural non-stick surface. Once again, this move was on the premise of "why mess around with the unknown if you don't have to?" Cast iron cookware, while not perfectly non-stick, is an option involving fewer questionable areas. We also employ stainless steel, glass and clay pots, pans and bake ware regularly.

HOMESCHOOL

We (Tina predominately) homeschool Matthew. We've found this to be the most suitable arrangement for his temperament. We may keep him out of mainstream schools until he reaches high-school age. He is quite smart, but he is not socially aware in most situations. This makes him easy prey for other children. Given the time and other constraints, homeschooling seems our best option. In school he was teased unceasingly, even in private Christian schools. He started out in a special-needs preschool in England, went on to a public school in North Carolina (where he had an IEP) and eventually to private Christian schools in NC an Arizona. In Arizona, we pulled him out. With his lack of social awareness, I doubt if he really understood that he was being teased.

At twelve years of age, Matthew is preparing to return to mainstream schooling. Rapidly approaching six-feet tall, he is at least on par, if not ahead of his peers physically and academically.

My main objection to mainstream school: their insistence that he read something he didn't want to read. Matthew wanted to read marine biology books (especially about cephalopods). The school insisted he be forced to read fiction. My opinion: what a fine way to develop and nurture a life-long hatred of reading in a child who wants to read. I explained my feeling on the matter and negotiated a deal with the school to allow Matthew to read more science books. I learned a lot about education from this.

We found it only takes about four hours for Tina to get Matthew through most of his daily lessons. The remainder of the time spent in a mainstream school is extraneous material. In homeschool, it is quieter, with fewer distractions. Difficult subjects requiring more concentration (math, language, reading and science) can be presented during Matthew's peak-learning hours. (For some reason, our schools insist on teaching nice-to-know subjects in class, and send home the critical subjects when the child is exhausted from a day in school.) This gives our son more playtime or time for his special studies in marine biology. Homeschooling brings a special benefit for us: there is less opportunity for the accidental introduction of forbidden foods into his diet.

Matthew also attended the Tucson Alliance for Autism's Social Skills Classes. I credit these classes with giving Matthew sufficient social skills to allow his autism to go undetected most of the time. I have no scientific evidence for this; I get an occasional, "he seems normal to me," comment from people he meets.

STORES IN TUCSON

Tucson is an excellent city for an all-natural GFCF diet. In North Carolina, we had to drive two hours to get to an organic/natural food store like The

Whole Foods Market. In Tucson, we were surrounded by them: Wild Oats, Sunflower Market, New Life and the list went on.

We also found a local store with a wide selection of teaching aids that allow us to customize Matthew's education. Just how wide: I even found a teacher's guide for fifth grade marine biology.

GLUTEN FREE, CASEIN FREE DIET

WHEN WE STARTED the gluten free casein free diet, my wife and I agreed we would eat whatever Matthew ate. Since Matthew's communication abilities were initially limited, we used ourselves as guinea pigs with the idea: Even though our diet was reviewed by a nutritionist, if a food or supplement bothered us, we would remove it from the family menu. If it upset one of our systems, it might have been upsetting Matthew's and he was unable to tell us. As the magnesium and B6 brought on increased communication, this became less of an issue but we still eat the same diet together.

BONUS BENEFIT

Special bonus benefit of Matthew's diet for adults: we each lost about 30 lbs without trying. This result was verified when I deployed for the initial assault on Iraq in 2003. Naturally, my entire diet when from organic GFCF to MRE's (Meal, Ready-to-Eat. A combat fast-food meal) and chow hall food. I gained back everything I lost. On my return home to the GFCF diet, I once again lost the 30 lbs while eating ice cream, chocolate, cookies and cakes (this sounds like a tabloid-diet pitch, but it's true).

I also feel much better despite my advancing age. I am healthier and suffer from fewer illnesses and ailments than previously. I seem to have better muscle tone, and I think my hair is growing back!

I don't want people to see this as a cure-all for all modern health problems, but I must mention my wife's allergies. Tina, a life-long allergy sufferer has stopped taking her medication with no ill effects after several years of restricted, natural diets. Among her specific allergens tumbleweed, mold and pine trees caused her much suffering. Today, however she resides in Tucson without the benefit of medication, an area where she is heavily exposed to all of those.

For the adults, we switched from coffee to a variety of organic teas. Our current favorite is Stash's Earl Gray Black and Green Tea. We have also determined certain dry wines are fine and easily available most places. Whiskey, Vodka and Gin, though made from wheat, do not have gluten remaining after distillation. Beer, unfortunately, is right out. A good Cider makes a fine alternative if you can find it. Before we went on the SCD diet, I did have a nice buckwheat ale called "Sara." Cost was a factor though. During a stay in Africa, I had some very good sorghum beer. Unfortunately, upon my return to the US, I was told it was unavailable in the US. Lately (2007), it has appeared in stores and on the internet. Some examples are Redbridge (by Anheuser-Busch) and Bard's Tale Dragon's Gold.

In an odd little aside, I began to wonder just why preservatives and other artificial ingredients were added to certain foods. We searched quite a while trying to find olives and pickles that didn't have a laundry list of unreadable names in the ingredients. We finally found Krinos olives (from Greece!) which contained nothing but olive, water, salt and olive oil. Amazingly, the shelf life was at least six months from the time of purchase and I never had any go bad in the refrigerator, all without the help of artificial ingredients. We even have nitrate-free bacon.

Recently (2007), we introduced goat dairy products into Matthew's diet. It took us a while to decide on goat dairy products, but based on our good experience with SCD, and some research on the difference between goat and cow casein, we went ahead with it. We have met with no detrimental effects thus far.

My Theory

NEANDERTHALS

When I first read about the GFCF diet I began to suspect some individuals were not adapted to eat everything they came across. I noted foods containing gluten and foods containing casein seem to be from an agricultural period of our history. Prior to the advent of agriculture, primitive man wouldn't have access to grains nor milk the primary sources of gluten and casein. Everything else, meats, eggs, fruit, vegetables (tubers) would be available to primitive foragers wandering around the countryside. For protein, they probably caught and killed small prey on occasion and supplemented this with eggs from the nests they came across. They gathered fruit as they moved following their prey and dug up tubers when time permitted.

AGRICULTURE

Once agriculture came on the scene and became our primary source of sustenance, problems with certain unnatural foods surfaced. Not everyone could eat grains and milk. Probably dismissed as "possessed by demons," these individuals and their odd behavior were marginalized by mainstream society. After the candle in the dark lit up, and mankind was given a few centuries to think about it, we were able to discover the cause. Others have this same idea and have called it the "Paleo-Diet."

ABOUT MATTHEW

Matthew is a 10 year old boy (now 12) diagnosed with high-functioning autism (HFA). His story began in 1995. Growing up his progress was relatively normal until he was two years old. At that point he began to regress. It seemed he was rapidly losing skills and abilities he had already mastered.

Part of the HFA syndrome is the laser-like mental focus the patients have for a single, often odd, topic/subject. As Matthew grew older, this single-mindedness was targeted on marine biology, specifically cephalopods. Matthew voraciously consumed all data, books and videos about squid and octopus. His idol is a marine biologist he saw in an octopus documentary, Mike DeGruys of the University of Arizona. Now, Matthew is dead-set on attending U of A in addition to the College of Oceaneering, a technical diving school in California. From a parent's point of view, this dedication to education is great, but it seems unnatural in a 10-year-old.

Far from locked into an unalterable routine, Matthew focus on Marine biology seems to be able to overcome the need for routine. Presented the opportunity to take scuba-diving lessons, he leapt at the chance. I assumed the first time he actually went under water, he would immediately resurface and want nothing to do with scuba. Instead, Matthew spent 30-minutes underwater, like he was born to it. He has already completed the PADI Seal Team's five Aqua-missions and is entering the Master Seal Program to continue his training.

We first began to suspect something was seriously wrong while we were living in England. (I was stationed at RAF Mildenhall with the U.S. Air Force.). Finally, Matthew's Red Cross swim instructor at RAF Lakenheath recognized his symptoms and tipped us off (her grandchildren had autism). Unfortunately, we were unable to get satisfactory medical care in the military, overseas. The military's immediate response, without even looking at him: medicate with the most powerful chemicals we can get our hands on. This justifiably frightened my wife and me. We quickly considered and rejected this option as it seemed the medical community was less well-informed than we were, and only guessing.

LIST OF MATTHEW'S SYMPTOMS:

Non-verbal

Repeating/copying:	Matthew would repeat whatever we said, sometimes phrased as a question.
Movie Scripts:	he seemed to be able to recite extensive portions or movie scripts from memory, mostly Disney animated. He would use portions of these as attempted "conversation."
Planned conversation:	he would repeat conversations over and over. He would often begin with a question he knew the answer to in order to get a predetermined response from the listener, and then go from there with another question (he knew the answer to this one too).
Stimming:	he would hold one or both hands near his mouth with the fingers pointing outward very rigidly (was this an early attempt to get words to come out of his mouth?) Today,

	when alone and quiet you may still see him looking at his hands in his lap, fingers rigid. If he realizes he is being watched, he stops. When questioned, he is unable to explain it.
Hand Flapping:	when running and excited.
Unable to toilet train	(until two months on GFCF diet)
Head banging	
Temper tantrums	
Inappropriate response to pain	
Speech:	today, his speech is still stilted and odd.

Today (2007), we see very little of these symptoms. Matthew is still socially awkward in some situations, but making progress with each new encounter.

DIAGNOSIS

Cumberland County Schools in North Carolina diagnosed Asperger's Syndrome while the University of Arizona went with high functioning autism. It was important to finally have a diagnosis. It was important to have a name to pin on the problem. Initially we were unaware of the need for a name. I think we didn't realize how much stress not having a name was generating. When we finally did have a name, it was a great relief for some reason. Anyway, I found the distinction between Asperger's and HFA frustrating. I have some experience in aviation diagnosing aircraft problems but I floundered when using the diagnostic tools for the autism spectrum (Hey! I'm not a doctor!).

There were very slight distinctions between the two. I would read through the diagnostic criteria once and choose Asperger's, read it again, and choose HFA. To make matters worse, professionals debated the existence of Asperger's as a separate diagnosis. Since a diagnosis of Asperger's is not recognized in Arizona, the sufferer has no entitlement to any support or assistance in that state. We opted for Autism since it is more widely accepted than Asperger's.

Due to our two main advantages (lots of observation and an unwillingness to risk the side effects of drugs), we felt our ideas of treatment couldn't be any worse than theirs and might even be more appropriate. Thus began a six-year, ongoing research project into Autism, diet, special equipment, therapy, classes and anything else we could find out about Autism and ways to deal with it. Far from being critical of the medical community at the time (they could not diagnose the problem), we felt our intense observation resulted in an equally intense level of knowledge in regard to Matthew's individual situation. It was simply impossible to convey our entire data in a comprehensible fashion to a physician in a 20-minute appointment.

DRUG THERAPIES

Our main objection to drug intensive therapies as a response to Autism: It seems we are bombarded weekly with sad tales of a person's life-long exposure to a particular substance originally deemed safe for exposure/ consumption. In the beginning, the medical community or other authority approved the substance in question for long term exposure (or short term exposure at a critical juncture, like Thalidomide) for the patient, worker or test subject. After 20 years pass the six-o'clock evening news' story is about the individual now suffers from cancer, kidney failure, etc. because he consumed a supposedly safe substance for 20 years.

How does this happen? To be honest, there is little that researchers can do. The best scientific method and statistical analysis can only provide a *probability* of a medication's safety, long or short term. Obviously, they will be more accurate short term (some unfortunates will still suffer debilitating, immediate side-effects, but their numbers will be statistically acceptable. As the length of treatment increases, accuracy of safety predictions drop off dramatically; who can accurately predict the entire future? Consequently, I believe long term use of today's approved drugs will *probably* result in future horror stories of premature death and disease, unforeseeable consequences of medicine's good-faith efforts to reduce suffering.

Please keep in mind: I am not a doctor, nor have I played one on TV. I am, however the dedicated father of a son with a problem. I am duty bound to find the best possible solution/support/therapy to cure/alleviate/adapt to for his particular position on the Autism spectrum. In consequence, I have spent years analyzing and researching proposed treatments. In some cases, I discard a particular theory/therapy because Matthew's symptoms differ significantly from the subject diagnosed in the research. On other occasions I have rejected research for lack of scientific rigor. While I have no formal medical training, my education allows me to identify well-planned and executed research and statistical analysis. It also helps me zero in on a researcher's particular weakness (often a formal limitation addressed in the research), and determine its impact on the quality of that research and its applicability to my son. I have also found research to be based solely on anecdotal evidence (one mother against the world) and tried it since it could have little in the way of side effects (What the Hell scenario). Based on the above self-imposed criteria, we attempted the Specific Carbohydrate Diet; returning to a simpler diet without losing anything of nutritional import would certainly coincide with the popular opinion that a doctor's first duty is to do no harm, with which I wholeheartedly agree (he is my son after all).

Conclusion

We completed our year on the scd diet and immediately reverted to the gfcf diet. There was much rejoicing.

It's been about a year since we completed our scd adventure. In the words of Horatio Nelson Jackson, "We expect to make good progress tomorrow."

This is not a self help book; I don't believe in them. They usually prescribe a single solution or antidote to all sufferers of a particular problem. ("If you do my diet and my exercises you will lose weight/ grow hair/ gain muscle or whatever you want," and it only ends up working for a few members of the audience.) This book is a record of some of our experiences and what worked for us. My policy is: Do whatever you want; I don't care.

Matthew knows he will never be able to eat at fast food places again. When we are in a big hurry it's inconvenient but he knows why. He knows he didn't talk much before the diet. We have never tricked him about food. For the last two years he has started to learn how to read food labels for himself and make good choices. So he can be independent and go to college.

On to the Recipes!

COOK'S NOTES

GINGER IS A warming spice that aids in digestion. I try to use it often.

Oil means olive oil unless otherwise stated. Especially when doing GFCF recipes the oil chosen can make a great deal of difference in the end product. An example personally done is brownies made with corn oil were dry and crumbly but the same brownies made with olive oil were moist. The same applies to margarine made with corn and margarine made with soy.

"Eggs" refer to US Grade Large (standard for cooking in US).
1 US Large egg= 1.5 fluid ounces= 1.75 ounces= 50 grams.
1 egg white= 2 tablespoons= 30 grams.
1 egg yolk= 1 tablespoon= 20 grams.

Honey means Clover Honey. It has a mild flavor that does not overpower other flavors in your food. Different types of honey have different water contents. That will affect your results.

Always measure the oil first then the honey and the honey will flow out of the measuring cup easy. If no oil is used in the recipe then spray it with olive oil first before measuring the honey.

Some gelatins are 1 tsp. envelopes and some are 2 tsp. envelopes so check!

British Cooking info at www.recipes4us.co.uk

All temperatures for the recipes in this book are in Fahrenheit. There are conversion charts at the end of the book for those who need to make changes.

For those who are only GFCF Guar Gum can substitute for Xanthan Gum in equal amounts in any recipe.

Buy an empty pump mister from a kitchen supply store and filled it with olive oil to spray pans with.

For those who can have goat dairy products just substitute the goat product in place of the rice milk, margarine, and cheese.

We try very hard to use as much organic ingredients as possible including meat.

The best thing I've found for cooking bacon is the "as seen on TV" Bacon Wave available from www.mileskimball.com and a white mesh splatter net. Then there is little to no clean up mess after.

Time saving tip: buy two packages of bacon at a time and cook both. After cooking, roll one of the packages up in paper towels, put it in a plastic bag and stick it in the freezer. Then when needed to steam vegetables, bake beans, or make pizza the bacon is ready to use.

Time saving tip: buy an extra jar of pickles for relish and just chop the whole jar at one time. Then, the next time you make a recipe calling for chopped pickles it's already done. Bubbies Dill Relish is great if it's available locally.

All brand names had been checked to verify ingredients before this was sent for publication as SCD or GFCF. It is the consumer's responsibility to verify all ingredients before use. Personally, we routinely check ingredients in the store aisle as we're shopping. We've found several trusted products in which the ingredients changed dramatically, without notice.

EQUIPMENT NOTES AND FAVORITES
14 cup capacity Cuisinart® with 3/4 h.p. motor
5 qt KitchenAid® Stand Mixer
5 qt Rival® Crock Pot
Nesco American Harvest® Dehydrator with six trays
Lodge Logic® cast iron cookware
Pampered Chef® clay bakeware
Calphalon® stainless steel cookware
Oxo® liquid measures
Candy thermometer
Progressive® nut grinder (hand-operated)
Mr. Mister by Norpro®
Carousel microwave 1.58 kW

BREADS,
CAKES
AND
COOKIES

Basic Muffins (SCD)

2 lg. Eggs
½ c. Clover Honey
2 c. Applesauce unsweetened or 1–23 oz. Jar
¼ c. Olive Oil
1 tsp. Calcium Powder
1 tsp. Baking Soda
6 c. Almond Flour
1 1/3 c. Walnuts chopped or other nuts
1 c. Fruit dried (blueberries, dates, cherries) Just Cherries

Place all the dry ingredients in a large bowl (except the dried fruit) and stir lightly to mix. Then add all the wet ingredients with the applesauce last. Stir to mix well, then add the dried fruit and stir again. Spoon into paper lined muffin tins. Bake at 310 degrees for 30–35 minutes. Test with a toothpick. It should be clean and dry. Cool on a wire rack.

Makes 24 muffins.

For Coconut add 1 c. coconut and subtract 1 c. almond flour.

For Pumpkin add 1–15 oz. can of pumpkin and only 1/3 c. applesauce, 1 tsp. cinnamon, and 1 tsp. nutmeg.

For Cinnamon add 2 tsp. of cinnamon ground.

For Ginger add 2 tsp. of ginger ground.

For Pineapple Cashew add 1 c. pineapple dried – Just Pineapple and chopped cashews.

Non-SCD: For Chocolate add 1 c. cocoa powder.

Non-SCD: For Chocolate Coconut add 1 c. cocoa powder and 1 c. coconut then subtract 1 c. almond flour.

Bread (SCD)

5 c. Almond Flour

1 1/3 c. Natural Peanut Butter or other nut butter

½ c. Ginger Ale–Dr. Tima Natural Ginger Ale with Honey

7 lg. Eggs

1 tsp. Baking Soda

1 tsp. Sea Salt

1 tsp. Calcium Powder

Place all the dry ingredients into a large bowl and stir lightly. Add all the wet ingredients and stir well. Pour into a sprayed loaf pan. Bake at 325 degrees for 60–75 minutes. Let the bread cool for 10 minutes then, remove the bread from the loaf pan to finish cooling on a wire rack.

Leftover Pumpkin Cake (SCD)

2 c. Nut Milk Solids – Leftovers from Nut Milk
1½ c. Pumpkin Filling – Leftovers from Pumpkin Pie
2/3 c. Clover Honey
2 lg. Eggs
3½ c. Almond Flour
1/3 c. Olive Oil
1 tsp. Calcium Powder
1½ tsp. Baking Soda
1 tsp. Cinnamon
1/3 c. Lemon Juice – Last!

Place all the dry ingredients into a bowl and stir well. Then add the wet ingredients. Place the Lemon Juice in Last. Mix well. Pour into a sprayed 9"x13" baking dish. Bake at 325 degrees for 45–60 minutes. Let the cake cool completely before icing or drizzle with honey after serving onto plates.

Meringue Cookies (SCD)

½ c. Just Whites powder Deb El
½ c. Orange Juice pure or other juice Warmed
(30 seconds on medium in microwave).
1/8 tsp. Sea Salt
1 c. Clover Honey
1 tsp. Orange Extract Flavorganics

In a large mixer bowl, dissolve egg whites in the warm juice for about 2 minutes. Stir lightly to get the lumps out. Beat on medium until frothy. Add the salt and the extract. Beat on high adding the honey gradually until very stiff peaks form. Line a baking sheet with parchment paper. Use a decorator's bag with a star type tip. Fill the bag with the meringue twist the open end closed. Squeeze from the top of the bag and make quarter-sized cookies. Release pressure to finish each cookie to a point. Bake at 200–225 degrees for approximately 2 hours.

Change the juice and the extract to come up with other flavors like mint, almond, and vanilla. Just remember no Agave syrup in the extract for SCD. We did blueberry too.

Pancakes (SCD)

1¼ c. Almond Flour

4 lg. Eggs

2 Tbsp. Clover Honey

2 tsp. Vanilla Extract or cinnamon, peppermint, etc...

¼ tsp. Sea Salt

¼ tsp. Baking Soda

½ tsp. Calcium Powder pure, Kirkman

Place all the dry ingredients into a bowl and stir lightly. Then add all the wet ingredients and stir again. Ladle the batter onto an oiled frying pan or griddle to make pancakes. Use medium heat to cook the pancakes. Watch them closely.

Serving size three pancakes. Serves 3.

Spice Cake (SCD)

1 tsp. Cinnamon ground pure

¼ tsp. Nutmeg ground

¼ tsp. Cloves ground

¼ tsp. Ginger ground

1 tsp. Calcium Powder Kirkman

4 c. Almond Flour

2 tsp. Baking Soda

½ tsp. Sea Salt

4 lg. Eggs

½ c. Olive Oil or other oil

1 c. Clover Honey

1/3 c. Orange Juice

Place all the dry ingredients into a bowl and stir lightly. Then add the wet ingredients (except the juice) and stir again. Add the orange juice in and stir again. Pour into a sprayed 9"x13" baking dish. Bake at 325 degrees for 45–60 minutes. Let the cake cool completely before icing or drizzle with honey after serving onto plates.

Three Berry Cake (SCD)

4 c. Almond Flour

1 tsp. Calcium Powder Kirkman

2 tsp. Baking Soda

½ tsp. Sea Salt

2 tsp. Gelatin unflavored unsweetened

¾ c. Strawberry Powder–Just Strawberries 1.5 oz. dried puree into powder

½ c. Safflower Oil or other oil

1 1/3 c. Clover Honey

4 lg. Eggs

1/3 c. Cranberry Juice Cons. R.W. Knudsen

Place all the dry ingredients together in a large mixing bowl and stir.

Then add all the wet ingredients. Beat 2 minutes on a medium speed. Pour into a sprayed 9"x13" baking dish. Bake at 325 degrees for about 50 minutes. When completely cooled, ice with Honey Acres Raspberry Honey Creme. Then refrigerate.

*I recently found another honey called billybee Spreadable Honey. It seems to be about the same consistency and should also work for this recipe. It is unflavored so adding just a few drops of Loran Natural Oils or a small amount like a ½ tsp. of a pure extract to flavor for icing.

Applesauce Cookies (SCD/GFCF)

1/3 c. Coconut Oil solid
2/3 c. Clover Honey
1 c. Applesauce
1 tsp. Baking Soda
1 lg. Egg beaten
½ tsp. Cinnamon ground
½ tsp. Nutmeg ground
½ tsp. Sea Salt
1 tsp. Calcium Powder Kirkman
2½ c. Almond Flour
1 c. Walnuts chopped
1 c. Raisins

Optional GFCF
1/3 c. Shortening Spectrum
1½ c. White Rice Flour
½ c. Sweet Rice Flour
1 tsp. Xanthan Gum or Guar Gum

Cream the coconut oil and honey together. Stir the soda with the applesauce, add the well-beaten egg. Combine with the creamed mixture. Add the flour and other dry ingredients, mix well. Add a little more flour if needed. Add the raisins and the walnuts. Drop by a spoon onto a greased baking sheet. Bake at 350 degrees for 20 minutes. Place the cookies on a wire rack to cool before storing in an airtight container.

Date Cookies (SCD/GFCF)

¼ c. Goat Butter, melted

2 c. Almond Flour

½ c. Dates pitted, chopped fine

1/3 c. Honey Spreadable billybee

1 tsp. Ginger ground

1 tsp. Calcium Powder

¼ tsp. Baking Soda

1/8 tsp. Sea Salt

Optional GFCF

¼ c. Margarine Earth Balance Buttery Sticks, melted

In a medium mixing bowl place the melted butter and all the rest of the ingredients except the flour and stir. Then add the flour and stir again. Using soup spoons, place a well rounded spoonful of dough onto a clay baking sheet and flatten a little with the back of one of the spoons. Bake at 275 degrees for approximately 25 minutes.

This recipe yields 1 dozen large cookies.

This recipe contains goat casein which is different from cow casein. Check with your doctor first to see if goat casein is acceptable for you.

Almond Pound Cake (GFCF)

1 roll Almond Paste Odense chopped into small pieces

1 c. White Sugar or ½ c. Clover Honey

1 c. Margarine GFCF like Willow Run

4 lg. Eggs

½ c. Milk Substitute like Soy Silk

1 tsp. Baking Powder

1 c. Almond Flour

½ c. Sweet Rice Flour

½ c. White Rice Flour

1 tsp. Xanthan Gum or Guar Gum

1 tsp. Calcium Powder Kirkman

Place the almond paste, sugar, and the margarine into a large mixing bowl and beat on medium speed until fluffy. Add the eggs one at a time and mix after each one. In a separate bowl place all the dry ingredients and stir to mix. Add the flour mix alternately with the milk to the creamed mix. Mix until the batter is smooth. Pour into a sprayed bundt pan. Bake at 325 degrees for 60 minutes. Cool the cake for 10 minutes then, remove the cake from the bundt pan. Finish cooling the cake on a wire rack. Glaze, ice, or drizzle chocolate or caramel syrup over it.

Basic Buttercream Icing (GFCF)

1/3 c. Shortening or Margarine Stick
1 lb. Powdered Sugar Miss Roben's corn-free
3 oz. Rice Milk Pacific or 1/3 c. + a little
1 Tbsp. Vanilla Extract or Mint, Orange, etc...
¼ tsp. Sea Salt
2 Tbsp. Sweet Rice Flour
1½ tsp. Lemon Juice
Natural Food Coloring like India Tree

Place all the ingredients into a large mixing bowl and beat at a low speed for 5 minutes. This recipe makes enough icing for a 9"x13" sheet cake.

Basic Muffins (GFCF)

1¼ c. Brown Rice Flour

1¼ c. White Rice Flour

1¼ c. Sweet Rice Flour

2 tsp. Xanthan Gum or Guar Gum

1 tsp. Baking Powder

1 tsp. Baking Soda

1 tsp. Calcium Powder

1 1/3 c. Walnuts finely chopped or other nuts

1 c. Fruit dried (blueberries, dates, cherries) Just Cherries

2 lg. Eggs

¼ c. Olive Oil

½ c. Clover Honey

2 c. Applesauce unsweetened or 1–23 oz. jar

Place all the dry ingredients in a large bowl (except the dried fruit) and stir lightly to mix. Then add all the wet ingredients with the applesauce last. Stir to mix well, then add the dried fruit and stir again. Spoon into paper lined muffin tins. Bake at 350 degrees for 20–25 minutes. Test with a toothpick. It should be clean and dry. Let cool on a wire rack.

Makes 24 muffins.

For Coconut add 1 c. coconut flakes and subtract either the nuts or the fruit.

For Double Chocolate Chip add ½ c. Cocoa powder and subtract ¼ c. of the brown and white rice flour, add chocolate chips and subtract the dried fruit.

For Cinnamon add 2 tsp. cinnamon ground.

For Ginger add 2 tsp. ginger ground.

For Pineapple Cashew add 1 c. pineapple dried–Just Pineapple and chopped cashews.

For Pumpkin add 1–15 oz. can of pumpkin and only 1/3 c. applesauce, 1 tsp. cinnamon, and 1 tsp. nutmeg.

Blueberry Icing (GFCF)

12 oz. Blueberry Jam or other flavor
1 tsp. Sea Salt
½ c. Coconut Oil in liquid form (melt if necessary)
1 c. Clover Honey
1½ c. Chestnut Flour

Blend well with an electric mixer. Ice the cake with a wet knife if necessary. Refrigerate after icing.

Brown Bread (GFCF)

2½ c. Brown Rice Flour

½ c. Sweet Rice Flour

1 Tbsp. Xanthan Gum or Guar Gum

1 Tbsp. Baking Powder

1 tsp. Sea Salt

1 tsp. Calcium Powder Kirkman

¾ tsp. Dough Enhancer

2 Tbsp. Olive Oil

2 lg. Eggs slightly beaten

1 1/3 c. Sparkling Water

2 Tbsp. Clover Honey

2 Tbsp. Molasses

Place all the dry ingredients in a bowl and stir lightly to mix. Place all the wet ingredients in a large mixing bowl (except the sparkling water) and beat on low. Add the dry ingredients to the wet ingredients and beat on low gradually adding the sparkling water in. Mix only until well combined. Pour into a sprayed loaf pan. Bake at 350 degrees for about 55 minutes. Test with a toothpick should be dry in the center. Cool the bread for 10 minutes then, remove it from the loaf pan to finish cooling on a wire rack.

Brownies, Cake-Like (GFCF)

2/3 c. Clover Honey
¾ c. Margarine Stick GFCF
½ c. Cocoa Powder unsweetened
2 lg. Eggs
1 tsp. Vanilla Extract
1 c. White Rice Flour
½ c. Sweet Rice Flour
1 tsp. Xanthan Gum or Guar Gum
1 tsp. Calcium Powder Kirkman

In a large saucepan, place the honey, margarine and the cocoa powder over medium heat until it melts, stirring continuously. Remove from heat. Add the eggs and the vanilla. Beat lightly until combined. Place all the dry ingredients together in a separate bowl and stir lightly. Add the dry ingredients and the milk alternately to the chocolate, beating after each addition. Pour batter into a sprayed 9"x13" baking dish. Bake at 350 degrees for 20 minutes.

Cherry Buttercream Icing (GFCF)

1/3 c. Shortening or Margarine Stick

1 lb. Powdered Sugar Miss Roben's corn-free

3 oz. Rice Milk Pacific or 1/3 c. + a little

1 Tbsp. Cherry Extract Frontier

½ tsp. Sea Salt

2 Tbsp. Sweet Rice Flour

1 Tbsp. Black Cherry Juice Concentrate pure unsweetened

In a large mixing bowl, combine all of the ingredients. Beat at a low speed for 5 minutes. This recipe makes enough icing for a 9"x13" sheet cake.

Cherry Chip Cake (GFCF)

3 c. White Rice Flour

1 c. Sweet Rice Flour

1 Tbsp. + 1 tsp. Baking Soda

1–3 oz. Cherry Jel Dessert Natural Desserts

1 tsp. Calcium Powder Kirkman

1 tsp. Xanthan Gum or Guar Gum

1–15 oz. can Pitted Cherries drained and chopped finely

1 c. Clover Honey

1 c. Black Cherry Juice Concentrate pure unsweetened

2 tsp. Cherry Extract Frontier

2 c. Canola Mayonnaise Spectrum 16 oz. size

Place all the dry ingredients together in a large mixing bowl and lightly stir. Then add all the wet ingredients to the dry mix. Beat for 2 minutes on a medium speed. Pour into a greased 9"x13" baking dish. Bake at 325 degrees for approximately 50 minutes. Test with a toothpick, it should be clean. Let the cake cool completely before icing.

Chocolate Buttercream Icing (GFCF)

1/3 c. Shortening or Margarine Stick
1 lb .Powdered Sugar Miss Roben's corn-free
3 oz. Rice Milk Pacific 1/3 c. + a little or Soy Silk Vanilla
¼ tsp. Sea Salt
1 Tbsp. Sweet Rice Flour
½ c. Cocoa Powder Unsweetened

In a large mixing bowl, combine all of the ingredients. Beat at low speed for 5 minutes. This recipe makes enough icing for a 9"x13" sheet cake.

Chocolate Cake (GFCF)

4 c. Chestnut Flour

1 tsp. Calcium Powder

1 Tbsp. + 1 tsp. Baking Soda

½ c. Cocoa Powder unsweetened

1 c. Clover Honey

1 c. Water

2 tsp. Vanilla Extract

2 c. Canola Mayonnaise – Spectrum 16 oz. size

1 tsp. Xanthan Gum or Guar Gum

1 tsp. Unflavored Gelatin

Put all the dry ingredients together in a large mixing bowl and lightly stir. Then add all the wet ingredients. Beat for 2 minutes on a medium speed. Pour into a sprayed 9"x13" baking dish. Bake at 325 degrees for approximately 50 minutes. Test with a toothpick, it should be clean. Let the cake cool completely before icing.

Chocolate Fudge Cake (GFCF)

3 c. White Rice Flour

1 c. Sweet Rice Flour

½ c. Cocoa Powder unsweetened

1 Tbsp. + 1 tsp. Baking Soda

1 tsp. Xanthan Gum or Guar Gum

1 tsp. Gelatin unflavored, unsweetened

1 tsp. Calcium Powder Kirkman

1 c. Clover Honey

1 c. Water

2 tsp. Vanilla Extract pure

2 c. Canola Mayonnaise Spectrum 16 oz. size

Place all the dry ingredients together in a large mixing bowl and lightly stir. Then, add all the wet ingredients. Beat for 2 minutes on a medium speed. Pour the batter into a greased 9"x13" baking dish. Bake at 325 degrees for approximately 50 minutes. Test with a toothpick, it should be clean. Let the cake cool completely before icing.

Chocolate Icing (GFCF)

2 sections Chocolate unsweetened Scharffen Berger
3–1 oz. bars Cocoa Butter Lorann Oils
1¾ c. Clover Honey
½ tsp. Sea Salt
1 tsp. Vanilla Extract
¾ c. Chestnut Flour
½ c. Coconut Oil

Put the coconut oil, cocoa butter, and chocolate into a double boiler, stirring constantly while melting. Remove from heat and add all the other ingredients. Stir really well to make sure that there are no lumps in it. Ice your cooled cake. I live in a hot climate so I kept mine in the refrigerator.

Chocolate Muffins (GFCF)

2½ c. Brown Rice Flour
½ c. Sweet Rice Flour
½ c. Cocoa Powder unsweetened
½ c. Rice Bran
2 Tbsp. Baking Powder
1 tsp. Xanthan Gum or Guar Gum
1 tsp. Baking Soda
½ tsp. Sea Salt
1 tsp. Calcium Powder Kirkman
2 c. Rice Milk or Soy Milk
4 lg. Eggs
¼ c. + 2 Tbsp. Olive Oil
2/3 c. Clover Honey
1 bag Chocolate Chips GFCF

Place all the dry ingredients into a large bowl and stir lightly. Whisk the eggs in a medium bowl. Then add the milk, oil, and the honey to the eggs and whisk again. Pour the liquid mixture into the dry mixture and stir to combine. Spoon batter into muffin tins lined with paper liners. Bake at 400 degrees for 18 minutes. Cool on a wire rack.

Makes 24 muffins.

Granny's Sugar Cookies (GFCF)

½ c. Margarine Earth Balance Stick or Goat Butter Meyenberg
1 c. White Sugar
1 lg. Egg
½ tsp. Sea Salt
2 tsp. Baking Powder Hain Featherweight
1 c. White Rice Flour
½ c. Sweet Rice Flour
½ c. Potato Starch
1 tsp. Calcium Powder Kirkman
2 tsp. Xanthan Gum
1 tsp. Vanilla Extract pure

Cream together the margarine and the sugar. Then blend in the egg and the vanilla. Next add all the rest of the dry ingredients and stir until well blended. Press the dough into a 9"x13" greased baking dish. Bake at 350 degrees for 20 minutes for a single batch. For a double batch of dough in one dish bake for approximately 25–30 minutes. Use a toothpick to test to see if it is done. Toothpick should be clean and dry. When cool sprinkle with cinnamon, sugar, and or spread with icing. Cut into bar cookies.

For variations change the extract to different flavors like mint, orange, cinnamon, etc...

This recipe contains goat casein which is different from cow casein. Check with your doctor first to see if goat casein is acceptable for you.

Molasses Cake (GFCF)

2 c. Brown Rice Flour

1 c. Sweet Rice Flour

1 tsp. Calcium Powder

1 tsp. Xanthan Gum

2 tsp. Baking Soda

1 tsp. Sea Salt

1 tsp. Ginger ground pure

1 tsp. Cinnamon ground pure

¾ c. Goat Milk evaporated Meyenberg

2½ tsp. Apple Cider Vinegar

1 c. Shortening Spectrum

1 c. Sugar natural

1 lg. Egg

½ c. Molasses Unsulphured Plantation

Nature's Colors Decorating Sugar India Tree (optional)

1 can Soy Whip Soyatoo (optional)

In a large mixing bowl, cream the shortening and the sugar together. Spray the measuring cup with olive oil before measuring the molasses for pour ability. Then, add the egg and molasses to the cream mixture and stir again. In a medium mixing bowl add all the remaining dry ingredients and stir lightly to mix. Combine the vinegar to the evaporated goat milk. Add the flour mix and the milk mixture to the creamed mixture. Stir again well and pour into a greased 9"x13" baking dish. Sprinkle with Nature's Colors Decorating Sugar (optional). Bake at 350 degrees for 20 minutes. Check with a toothpick. The toothpick should be clean. Spray individual servings with soy whip right before serving (optional).

*This recipe contains goat casein which is different from cow casein. Check with your doctor first to see if goat casein is acceptable for you.

Molasses Cookies (GFCF)

¾ c. Molasses Unsulphured

¾ c. Shortening Spectrum

2 lg. Eggs

1½ c. Brown Rice Flour

½ c. Sweet Rice Flour

¼ c. Potato Starch

1 tsp. Sea Salt

1 tsp. Baking Soda

1½ tsp. Cinnamon ground

½ c. Rice Milk or Goat Milk

1 tsp. Calcium Powder Kirkman

2 tsp. Xanthan Gum

½ tsp. Baking Powder

Beat the molasses into the shortening. Then add the eggs and beat again. Add the milk and the dry ingredients and beat well until mixed. Spread into a greased 9"x13" baking dish. Sprinkle with sugar if desired. Bake at 350 degrees for 30 minutes. Cool completely and cut into cookie bars.

This recipe contains goat casein which is different from cow casein. Check with your doctor first to see if goat casein is acceptable for you.

Royal Icing (GFCF)

2 tsp. Just Whites powder Deb El prepared as directed
2 Tbsp. Water for egg whites
1½ c. Powdered Sugar Miss Roben's corn-free
¼ tsp. Cream of Tartar
Lemon Juice a few drops
Vanilla Extract a few drops or Mint, Orange, etc...
Food Color a few drops India Tree

Place all the ingredients into a large mixing bowl and stir. Beat at highest speed for 10 minutes. Quickly spoon the icing into a decorator's bag. Squeeze directly onto mints, chocolate eggs, marshmallows, cookies, and cakes as stars, flowers, etc... Let dry over night. Squeeze any leftover icing onto parchment paper and let dry over night or longer before storing for later use. Store the left over decorations in an airtight container.

SOUP,
SALADS
AND
SALAD DRESSING

Chicken Salad (SCD)

2–10 oz. cans White Chicken in Water drained Valley Fresh
½ c. Celery finely chopped
¼ to ½ c. Dill Pickle chopped
2 lg. Eggs hard-boiled, chopped
¼ to ½ c. Canola Mayonnaise Spectrum
½ tsp. Sea Salt
¼ tsp. Paprika
¼ tsp. Garlic Powder
¼ tsp. Onion Powder

Mix all ingredients together well in a container with a lid. Refrigerate. Serve on bread or on a bed of your favorite salad greens.

Cucumber Salad (SCD)

Italian Salad Dressing (doubled)
2 Cucumbers medium sliced
½ c. Black Olives sliced Santa Barbara Olive Co.
1 Red Chile mild sliced (optional)
½ c. Onion chopped (optional)

Mix in a bowl with a lid. For better flavor let it set in the refrigerator overnight before serving.

Egg Salad Spread (SCD)

4 lg. Eggs hard-boiled, shelled
½ tsp. Mustard Annie's Naturals   Check Ingredients!
2 Tbsp. Canola Mayonnaise Spectrum
¼ tsp. Sea Salt

Place the eggs in a small bowl with a lid and chop them. Add all the other ingredients in and stir until mixed well. For variety add ¼ tsp. Onion Powder, ¼ tsp. Paprika, and or 2 strips of crispy bacon crumbled up in it. Serve on a bed of salad greens, bread, or almond crackers.

Ketchup (SCD)

1–6 oz. can Tomato Paste pure Muir Glen

½ c. Water

¼ c. Pear Sweet pure Wax Orchards or Honey

2 Tbsp. Apple Cider Vinegar

½ tsp. Sea Salt

¼ tsp. Onion Powder pure

In a bowl, whisk all ingredients together until there are no lumps in it. Store ketchup in a glass container with a lid and refrigerate.

Matthew's Lentil Soup (SCD)

1 lb. Red Lentils soaked, rinsed, and cooked for approximately 15 minutes
7 c. Water
¼ c. Onions dehydrated Just Onions
1 lb. Peas & Carrots frozen, thawed
1 lb. Lima Beans frozen, thawed
1½ tsp. Sea Salt
1 tsp. Garlic Powder
1 tsp. Sage
6 stripes Bacon cooked & crumbled

Put all the ingredients into a crock-pot and cook for 6 hours on high.

Pea Salad (SCD)

1 sm. pkg. Peas frozen, steamed & cooled
3 lg. Eggs hard-boiled, chopped
¼ c. Onion chopped optional
¼ c. Dill Pickles chopped
¼ c. Celery chopped
½ tsp. Sea Salt
2 Tbsp. Canola Mayonnaise Spectrum

Steam and cool the peas. Chop the hard-boiled eggs, onion, dill pickles, and the celery. Place all the ingredients into a medium bowl with a lid. Stir and chill in the refrigerator until needed.

Thousand Island Dressing (SCD)

1 c. Canola Mayonnaise Spectrum

¼ c. Ketchup

3 Tbsp. Dill Pickles, chopped Cascadian Farm

2 Tbsp. Parsley, chopped

1 Tbsp. Chives, chopped

1½ Tbsp. Clover Honey

½ tsp. Sea Salt

In a small bowl place all the ingredients and whisk. Pour into a small container with a lid. I like Rubbermaid's 1 pt. Pour-able Serve/Savers. Keep refrigerated. This recipe will last about one week in the refrigerator.

Tina's Cold Bean Salad (SCD)

1 lb. Navy Beans soaked, drained, cooked for 10 hours, and rinsed
½ c. Onions dehydrated Just Onions or fresh
1½ lbs. Chicken Strips, cooked and cut into bite size pieces
3–4 Dill Pickles, chopped Cascadian Farm
¼ c. Canola Mayonnaise Spectrum
¼ c. Yellow Mustard Annie's Naturals
1/8 tsp. Garlic Powder pure no fillers
1/8 tsp. Paprika
¼ tsp. Sea Salt

Cook the onions with the navy beans in a crock pot for 10 hours on low. Make sure the water is 1" over the top of the beans. Then rinse them. The beans can be done the day before. Add all the other ingredients and stir well. Refrigerate. Serve on a bed of your favorite salad greens.

Serves 6.

Beef Soup (SCD/GFCF)

2 c. Beef dehydrated Alpine Aire or fresh cooked
¼ c. Onion dehydrated Just Onions or fresh chopped
1–10 oz. Peas & Carrots frozen slightly thawed
1 c. Zucchini or Courgette sliced optional
1 tsp. Garlic chopped
½ tsp. Sea Salt
8 c. Water boiling
2 Tbsp. Paprika optional

Optional GFCF
1 large Potato peeled & diced
2 Tbsp. Worcestershire Sauce

Place all the ingredients into a crock-pot and cook on a high setting for 4 hours.

Chicken Soup (SCD/GFCF)

2 c. Chicken dehydrated Alpine Aire or fresh cooked
8 c. Water boiling
¼ c. Onion dehydrated Just Onions or fresh
1 c. Peas dehydrated Alpine Aire or fresh
2–14 oz. cans Chicken Broth Sheltons
1–4 oz. can Mushrooms sliced, drained
2 c. Carrots dehydrated Alpine Aire or fresh sliced
½ tsp. Sea Salt
1 tsp. Garlic chopped or powder
Paprika or Pepper to taste

Optional GFCF
2 cubes Vegetable Bouillon Rapunzel
2 c. Rice cooked

Place all the ingredients (except the rice optional) in a crock-pot and cook on a high setting for 4 hours. If using rice add it just before serving.

French Dressing (SCD/GFCF)

¾ c. Safflower Oil or Olive Oil

½ c. Clover Honey

¼ c. Apple Cider Vinegar or White Wine Vinegar

¼ c. Lemon Juice

¾ c. Ketchup

1 Tbsp. Sea Salt

½ tsp. Paprika

½ tsp. Onion Powder

½ tsp. Garlic Powder

½ tsp. Dry Mustard ground

Optional GFCF

¼ tsp. Xanthan Gum or Guar Gum

Put all the ingredients in a small container with a lid. I like Rubbermaid's 1 pt. Pour-able Serve/Savers. Shake until the honey is dissolved and it is mixed. Shake to remix before using each time. The dressing will last about one week in the refrigerator.

Italian Salad Dressing (SCD/GFCF)

1Tbsp. Garlic chopped

1 tsp. Sea Salt

½ c. Olive Oil

½ c. Safflower Oil or Olive Oil

2 Tbsp. Apple Cider Vinegar or White Wine Vinegar

¼ c. Lime Juice

¼ tsp. Oregano

¼ tsp. Black Pepper

Optional GFCF

¼ tsp. Xanthan Gum or Guar Gum

Mix all the ingredients together in a container with a lid. I like Rubbermaid's 1 pt. Pour-able Serve/Savers. Shake well to mix the dressing. Shake to remix before using each time. The dressing will last about one week in the refrigerator.

Russian Dressing (SCD/GFCF)

½ c. Safflower Oil or Olive Oil

½ c. Ketchup

2 Tbsp. Clover Honey

2 Tbsp. White Wine Vinegar

2 Tbsp. Lemon Juice

1 tsp. Paprika pure

½ tsp. Sea Salt

1/8 tsp. Black Pepper optional

Optional GFCF

¼ tsp. Xanthan Gum or Guar Gum

Put all the ingredients in a small container with a lid. I like Rubbermaid's 1 pt. Pour-able Serve/Savers. Shake until the honey is dissolved and it is mixed. Shake to remix before using each time. The dressing will last about one week in the refrigerator.

Turkey & Bean Soup (SCD/GFCF)

2 c. Turkey dehydrated or fresh cooked

1 c. Peas dehydrated or fresh

¼ c. Onions dehydrated or fresh chopped

8 c. Water boiling

½ tsp. Sea Salt

1 tsp. Garlic dehydrated or fresh chopped

1–6 oz. can Tomato Paste pure Muir Glen

1 tsp. Paprika optional

3–4 cups SCD prepared Beans optional

1 c. Celery sliced optional

Optional GFCF

1 large Potato diced

2–15 oz. cans Kidney Beans drained

1 tsp. Worcestershire Sauce GF

Place all the ingredients into a crock-pot and cook on a high setting for 4 hours.

Fruit Mellow Salad (GFCF)

2 c. Boiling Water
1–3 oz. Cherry Jel Dessert Natural Desserts
1 c. Ricemellow Creme Suzanne's
1–15.5 oz. can Pitted Cherries Columbia Gorge chopped
Chocolate Sprinkles Miss Roben's optional

Warm the can of cherries in hot water. Reserve a few of them for a garnish. After the can is warm, open and drain the cherries. Quickly chop the cherries while they are still warm. In a medium mixing bowl add boiling water to the Jel Dessert and whisk until it is dissolved. Then, add the ricemellow creme and whisk again. Next, add the chopped cherries and whisk again. Ladle into sundae glasses and refrigerate. Garnish with a half of a cherry and chocolate sprinkles.

Maple Dressing (GFCF)

1/3 c. White Wine Vinegar or Apple Cider Vinegar
½ c. Olive Oil or Safflower Oil
3 Tbsp. Maple Syrup pure
1 Tbsp. Mustard prepared Annie's Naturals
½ tsp. Garlic Powder pure
1/8 tsp. Black Pepper optional
1/8 tsp. Xanthan Gum

Put all the ingredients in a small container with a lid. I like Rubbermaid's 1 pt. Pour-able Serve/Savers. Shake until the mustard is dissolved and it is mixed. Shake to remix before using each time. The dressing will last about one week in the refrigerator.

Party Potato Salad (GFCF)

4 lg. White Potatoes peeled, cut into 8ths, boiled

2 med. Purple Potatoes peeled, cut into 4ths, boiled

¼ c. Sweet Onion chopped

2 lg. Eggs hard-boiled, coarsely chopped

9 slices Bacon cooked crisp and crumbled

1 tsp. Sea Salt

¾ tsp. Paprika

2 tsp. Mustard prepared Annie's Naturals

1 c. Canola Mayonnaise Spectrum

1 Tbsp. White Wine Vinegar Spectrum

2 Tbsp. Parsley Flakes

Peel, cut and boil the potatoes until cooked but still a little firm. If in a hurry after draining the potatoes rinse with cold water and let them set for just a few minutes. Then drain and slice the potatoes. In a container with a lid mix all the ingredients except the potatoes and stir well. Next add the potatoes and stir again. Store the potato salad in the refrigerator. Serve on a bed of your favorite salad greens. The salad can be topped with your favorite shredded cheddar cheese (Vegan Gourmet or Goat) or roasted and salted pumpkin seeds for a nice summer dinner.

*This recipe contains goat casein which is different from cow casein. Check with your doctor first to see if goat casein is acceptable for you.

Potato Soup (GFCF)

4 large Potatoes peeled and diced
10 stripes Bacon cooked and crumbled
½ c. Mashed Potato Flakes
8 c. Water boiling
½ c. Onion dehydrated or chopped
1 tsp. Thyme
1 tsp. Garlic Powder
1 tsp. Sea Salt
1 tsp. Paprika

2 Tbsp. Margarine Earth Balance Buttery Sticks melted
¼ c. Sweet Rice Flour
2 c. Rice Milk Pacific

Place the first set of ingredients into a crock-pot and cook on a high setting for 4 hours. After melting the margarine add the rice flour and stir into a paste. Then add the milk, stir and mash all the lumps out over medium heat. Stir constantly until it is thick and creamy. Then add it to the first mixture in the crock-pot and stir again. Continue simmering and stirring occasionally until the 4 hour cycle is completed.

Variation: Goat butter and goat milk can be used to substitute the margarine and the rice milk.

This recipe contains goat casein which is different from cow casein. Check with your doctor first to see if goat casein is acceptable for you.

Ranch Dressing (GFCF)

1 c. Canola Mayonnaise Spectrum

1 c. Rice Milk Pacific or Goat Milk evaporated

1 Tbsp. Lemon Juice

2 Tbsp. Chives freeze dried chopped

1 Tbsp. Parsley Flakes

¼ tsp. Garlic Powder

¼ tsp. Onion Powder

½ tsp. Paprika

½ tsp. Sea Salt

¼ tsp. Xanthan Gum

¼ tsp. Black Pepper optional

Put the lemon juice into the milk and let it stand for 10 minutes before using. In a small bowl place all the other ingredients and whisk. Then add the milk when it is finished standing and whisk again. Pour into a small container with a lid. I like Rubbermaid's 1 pt. Pour-able Serve/Savers. Shake to remix before using each time. The dressing will last about one week in the refrigerator.

*This recipe contains goat casein which is different from cow casein. Check with your doctor first to see if goat casein is acceptable for you.

ENTREES
AND
SAUCES

Chili Lime Sauce Mild (scd)

1/3 c. Lime Juice Santa Cruz
1/3 c. Clover Honey
½ tsp. Sea Salt
½ tsp. Chili Powder (...or more to your taste) pure no fillers
1 tsp. Ginger ground

Mix all the ingredients together in a small bowl and stir. Pour over steaks or your favorite meat and cook.

Cinnamon Sauce (scd)

1/3 c. *Plain Smooth Peanut Butter no additives*
1/3 c. *Clover Honey*
1/3 c. *Water*
1¼ tsp. *Sea Salt*
1 tsp. *heaping Cinnamon ground pure*

Put all the ingredients into a small container with a lid (like Rubbermaid's 1 pt. Pour-able Serve/Savers) and shake well until mixed. Great on seared Chicken strips. To make it thicker reduce the water a little for a spread. Add a little extra water to thin for a wonderful salad dressing.

Chili (SCD)

1 lb. Kidney Beans soaked, drained, cooked for 4 hour on high, and rinsed

1 lb. Ground Turkey browned

32 oz. Tomato Juice unsweetened R.D. Knudsen

2–3 c. Carrots chopped

½ c. Onions dehydrated Just Onions or fresh chopped

3 c. Water

1½ tsp. Sea Salt

1 tsp. Garlic

1 tsp. Chili Powder

Put all the ingredients into a crock-pot and cook for 6 hours on high. Add more water if needed.

Fried Chicken Coating (SCD)

2 c. Almond Flour
1 tsp. Sea Salt
1 tsp. Onion Powder pure no fillers
1 tsp. Garlic Powder
1 tsp. Paprika
1 tsp. Thyme

1¼ lbs. Chicken Strips
Olive Oil
1 lg. Egg slightly beaten

Put all the dry ingredients in an airtight container and shake until mixed well. Depending on how much chicken is being cooked it takes about a ½ c. of the coating mix. Use two narrow shallow dishes. One dish for a beaten egg and the other dish for the coating mix. Place one piece of the chicken in the beaten egg first on both sides. Then place the piece of chicken in the coating mix on both sides and fry in olive oil. Do not reuse any of the coating mix that has come into contact with raw meat.

Oven BBQ Ribs (SCD)

3–4 lbs. Pork country style ribs boneless
1 bottle Sweet Black Cherry BBQ Sauce

Oil a 9"x13" baking dish and place the meat in it. Bake at 425 degrees for 45 minutes uncovered. Then, drain all juices and check the doneness of the ribs. Pour BBQ sauce over the meat. Coat the meat well. Bake at 375 degrees for 30 minutes uncovered. Spoon the sauce back over the top of meat every 15 minutes until done. Cut a rib open to check for doneness. It should be white not pink in the center of the meat.

Serves 3 to 4.

Pizza Crust (SCD)

1½ c. Almond Flour + a little
3 lg. Eggs
1 tsp. Calcium Powder
1 Tbsp. Olive Oil
1 tsp. Sea Salt
1 tsp. Oregano
1 tsp. Garlic Powder
1 tsp. Onion Powder

In a bowl put all the dry ingredients and stir lightly. Then add all the wet ingredients and stir again. If needed add a little more almond flour. Spray a pizza pan with olive oil. I use a deep-dish clay baker. Pour a little olive oil on your hands and press the dough evenly onto the pan. I like the deep dish because then there is no bubble over mess to clean up. Bake at 350 degrees for about 15 minutes. Top with your favorite toppings. We like tomato sauce with thinly sliced cheese with cooked ground beef, crisp crumbled bacon, mushrooms, and black olive. It makes a cheeseburger pizza. Bake again about 15 minutes until done.

Shish Kabobs (scd)

1½ c. Olive Oil

½ c. White Wine Vinegar or Apple Cider Vinegar

2 Tbsp. Mustard dry ground

2 tsp. Parsley Flakes

2 tsp. Sea Salt

2 tsp. Paprika

1/3 c. Lemon Juice

1 tsp. Sage rubbed

1 tsp. Thyme

2 tsp. Garlic Powder

2 tsp. Onion Powder

2 tsp. Ginger ground

2½ lbs. Beef cubed

2 Bell Peppers any color cut into large chunks

1 bag Cherry Tomatoes washed

1 lg. Onion cut into large chunks

Mix all of the top ingredients in a 4–cup measuring cup. Whisk to mix. Reserve in a separate container approximately 1–cup for grilling or as a sauce after grilling. Place the meat and the rest of the marinade into a container with a lid and marinade for at least 6 hours or overnight. Place the meat, onion, pepper, and tomatoes onto skewers and grill for approximately 15 minutes turning once or until desired doneness. Do not reuse any of the marinade that has come into contact with raw meat.

Sloppy Joes (SCD)

1½ lbs. Ground Turkey browned or Beef
½ c. Onion chopped or more, optional
½ c. Sweet Black Cherry BBQ Sauce approximately
¼ c. Ketchup approximately

Brown the onions and meat in a large frying pan. Add the bbq sauce and ketchup. Stir until it is all moistened. Add more sauce or ketchup if needed. Eat plain or with bread like a sandwich.

Spaghetti Squash with Meat Sauce (SCD)

1 Spaghetti Squash
1 lb. Ground Turkey or other meat
1–24.5 oz. jar Marinara Sauce Amy's   Check Ingredients!
½ tsp. Garlic Powder pure optional
½ tsp. Onion Powder pure optional

Brown the meat in a large oiled frying pan. Then add the sauce and the spices. Stir and turn down the heat to let the sauce simmer while preparing the squash. Wash the squash, and then cut it in half lengthwise. Scoop out the seeds but not the meaty part like a pumpkin. In a large pot or dutch oven cover the bottom with about 1" of water then place a steaming rack flat in the bottom. Remove the stem to the steaming rack if you can. Place the squash in with the rind down next to the water and cover with a lid. Turn the squash onto high heat. When the water starts to boil start timing the squash for 15–20 minutes. Twenty minutes for a large squash. When the time is up remove it from the heat and uncover. Lift the squash onto a plate and use a fork to scrape spaghetti like strands from the squash onto serving plates then cover with sauce and serve.

Serves approximately 3 to 6.

Sweet and Sour Chicken (scd)

1½ lbs. Chicken Strips
1 c. Crushed Pineapple with its own juice
4 Tbsp. Red Wine Vinegar
¼ tsp. Ginger ground pure with no fillers
¼ tsp. Onion Powder
¼ tsp. Paprika
1½ tsp. Chives chopped
4 Tbsp. Clover Honey

Put all the ingredients in a small pot except the chicken. Stir and bring to a gentle boil then turn the heat down and let it simmer. Spray a frying pan with olive oil. Use medium/high heat and sear the chicken strips on both sides. Turn down the heat to just under medium. Pour the sauce over the chicken and continue to simmer. Cover with a lid but vent it. Continue to simmer until the chicken is finished cooking.

Serves 3.

Three Fish – Orange Fish (scd)

3 filets Tilapia or more or other mild white fish
¼ c. Clover Honey
½ c. Orange Juice with no additives
¼ c. Water
¼ tsp. Basil
½ tsp. Ginger ground pure no fillers

In a measuring cup or a small bowl, mix all the ingredients except the fish. Stir until the honey is completely dissolved. Spray a frying pan with olive oil. Sear the fish on both sides on a medium/high heat. Turn the heat down just under medium and pour the sauce over the fish. Let it gently boil until the sauce reduces down and gets thicker.

Serves 3.

Chicken Sandwiches (SCD/GFCF)

¼ lb. Cheddar Cheese cubed (Goat or Vegan Gourmet)

3 lg. Eggs hard-boiled, shelled, chopped

1–5 oz. can White Chicken Meat Valley Fresh

1 tsp. Green Pepper minced

1 tsp. Onion minced

3 Tbsp. Stuffed Green Olives chopped   Check Ingredients!

2 Tbsp. Dill Pickle Relish Bubbies

½ c. Canola Mayonnaise Spectrum

¼ tsp. Sea Salt

½ tsp. Garlic Powder pure

½ tsp. Paprika

Bread Slices SCD

Optional GFCF

Hot Dog Buns Kinnikinnick

Place the hard-boiled eggs into a medium mixing bowl and chop with a knife. Drain the chicken meat and add it to the eggs. Chop the remaining ingredients and also add them to the eggs and meat. Add the pickle relish, mayonnaise, and spices then stir well to mix. Place mixture on top of the bread or in the hot dog bun. Bake at 300 degrees for 15 minutes. This recipe can also be served cold on top of a bed of your favorite salad greens.

*This recipe contains goat casein which is different from cow casein. Check with your doctor first to see if goat casein is acceptable for you.

Easy Shrimp Supper (SCD/GFCF)

1½ lbs. Cooked Shrimp (Prawn) frozen 26/30 per lb.
1 lb. Peas frozen, thawed
1 c. Onion chopped, frozen or fresh
½ tsp. Garlic chopped or powder
½ tsp. Sea Salt
Paprika

Optional GFCF
1 envelope Rice frozen Rice Expressions, cooked or regular rice

Place frozen shrimp into a colander and run cold water over the shrimp for a quick thaw. Shake off excess water. Pull off the tails. Run cold water over the bag of frozen peas for a quick thaw. Place the shrimp, onions, and peas into a large frying pan with olive oil covering the bottom of the pan. Turn onto medium heat. Stir, then add the spices and stir again. Cook, stirring occasionally until completely thawed and excess water has evaporated, approximately 15-20 minutes. Then serve onto plates with a bed of rice or your favorite salad greens. Sprinkle with paprika and serve.

Serves 3-4.

Honey Mustard Pork Chops (SCD/GFCF)

3 Boneless Sirloin Chops or more

1/3 c. Yellow Mustard Annie's Naturals

1/3 c. Clover Honey

1/3 c. Safflower Oil or Olive Oil

1/3 c. Water

1 tsp. Ginger ground pure no fillers

1 tsp. Parsley

½ tsp. Sea Salt

Optional GFCF

¼ tsp. Xanthan Gum or Guar Gum

Put all the ingredients except the pork into a small container with a lid. Shake well until the honey has completely dissolved. Set aside. Spray a large frying pan with olive oil and put the pork chops in. Over medium/high heat, sear the pork chops on both sides. Then turn the heat down to just below medium. Pour sauce over the pork chops. Cover with a lid that is vented. Gently simmer and finish cooking the pork.

Serves 3.

Stew (SCD/GFCF)

1½ lbs. Stew Beef cubed and browned
1–6 oz. can Tomato Paste pure Muir Glen
1–10 oz. bag Peas & Carrots frozen, thawed
2 c. Onion chopped
1 tsp. Garlic chopped
1 tsp. Sea Salt
1 tsp. Thyme
1 tsp. Paprika
8 c. Water
1 c. Celery chopped optional
1 c. Zucchini chopped optional

Optional GFCF
1 lb. Potatoes fingerling washed
2 tsp. Xanthan Gum or Guar Gum

Brown the stew meat in a large frying pan. In a crock-pot dilute the tomato paste with 2 c. of the 8 c. of water. Then add the browned meat and the rest of the ingredients. Next add the remaining 6 c. of the water and stir well to mix. Set the crock-pot on high for 4 hours.

Sunday Roast (SCD/GFCF)

1½ lbs. Pork loin or Beef

2 Tbsp. Olive Oil

4 c. Water

½ c. Onions dehydrated Just Onions or fresh chopped

1 tsp. Garlic chopped Christopher Ranch Organic

1 tsp. Sea Salt

1 tsp. Sage

Optional GFCF

2–3 Tbsp. Sweet Rice Flour

½ c. Cold Water

Put the olive oil in a dutch oven and the meat. Sear the meat on all sides. Then add all the other ingredients except the sweet rice flour and ½ c. water. Bring it to a boil and then turn it down and let it simmer for about 4 hours. Remove the roast. Before serving add the sweet rice flour with the ½ c. cold water and stir. Then add it to the boiling broth slowly and stirring constantly until it thickens to make it gravy.

Sweet Black Cherry BBQ Sauce (SCD/GFCF)

¼ c. Safflower Oil or Olive Oil

¼ c. Clover Honey

¾ c. Ketchup

1/3 c. Black Cherry Juice Conc. R.W. Knudsen

2 Tbsp. Apple Cider Vinegar or White Wine Vinegar

1 tsp. Sea Salt

1 tsp. Onion Powder pure no fillers

1 tsp. Garlic Powder

1 tsp. Paprika

½ tsp. Oregano

Optional GFCF

¼ tsp. Xanthan Gum or Guar Gum

Put all the ingredients in a small container with a lid. I like Rubbermaid's 1 pt. Pour-able Serve/Savers. Shake it until the honey is completely dissolved and the sauce is mixed well. This recipe will last about one week in the refrigerator.

Taco Spice Mild (SCD/GFCF)

½ c. Chili Powder pure no fillers (or more to your taste)

½ c. Cumin ground

½ c. Oregano

¼ c. Paprika

½ c. Garlic Powder

½ c. Onion Powder

¼ c. Sea Salt

Optional GFCF

¼ c. Tapioca Starch so it will make a nicer sauce. Other possible ingredients are sweet rice flour, potato starch, and arrow root starch.

Mix all the ingredients together well in an airtight container with a lid. To use add 2 Tbsp. of the spice mix and a ½ c. of water to one pound of ground meat that has been browned. Stir and simmer the meat sauce until thickens. Add sliced black olives and or black beans. Serve on a bed of your favorite salad greens. The meat sauce can be topped with salsa and cheese (GFCF or Goat) if desired.

*This recipe contains goat casein which is different from cow casein. Check with your doctor first to see if goat casein is acceptable for you.

Batter Coating Mix (GFCF)

2/3 c. Garbanzo & Fava Flour Bob's Red Mill Mix

1/3 c. Potato Starch or other starch

½ tsp. Garlic Powder pure

½ tsp. Onion Powder pure

½ tsp. Baking Powder

½ tsp. Sea Salt

½ tsp. Oregano

1 tsp. Paprika

Place all the ingredients into a small container with a lid and shake or stir lightly with a spoon. This makes enough for approximately 2 or 3 uses with the oven fried chicken recipe. Never reuse any coating mix that has come into contact with raw meat.

Beef Broccoli Pie (GFCF)

1–9" Deep Dish Pie Shell Miss Roben's Pie Crust Mix

1 lb. Ground Beef lean browned

¼ c. Onion dehydrated Just Onions or fresh chopped

¼ c. Water to reconstitute the onions optional

1 tsp. Garlic chopped or Powder

½ lb. Chopped Broccoli frozen, thawed

1–8 oz. pkg. Cream Cheese Tofutti or 2–5.3 oz. Goat Cheese Chavrie

1 tsp. Worcestershire Sauce

½ tsp. Sea Salt

Prepare the piecrust according to the directions or use your own. While browning the ground beef, reconstitute the onions with the water. Then add the onions (do not drain) and the garlic to the beef. Poke holes in the bottom and side of the piecrust and pre-bake it for 10 minutes before filling it. Next, add the broccoli to the beef mixture. Stir and cook for about 5 minutes or so, especially if the broccoli was still partially frozen. Then add the cheese, sea salt, and Worcestershire sauce to the beef mixture. Turn the heat down to medium low and stir until the cheese is melted and smooth. Fill the pre-baked pie shell and bake for approximately 1 hour at 350 degrees.

Serves 4–8.

*Tip—For a quick thaw when you are running late. Put the broccoli into a strainer and run warm water over it, just until the broccoli breaks into pieces. Shake off the excess water.

This recipe contains goat casein which is different from cow casein. Check with your doctor first to see if goat casein is acceptable for you.

Broccoli Lasagna (GFCF)

1 lb. Ground Turkey lean

¼ c. Onions chopped or dehydrated reconstituted

1–24 oz. Marinara Sauce Amy's   Check Ingredients!

1–8 oz. Chopped Broccoli frozen, thawed

2–5.3 oz. Chavrie Goat Cheese or Cheese Substitute Ricotta

1 lg. Egg

1 pkg. Rice Lasagna Noodles DeBoles uncooked

1 tsp. Garlic chopped or Powder pure

1–7 oz. Cheddar Goat Cheese Meyenberg shredded or
Vegan Gourmet sliced very thin

Brown the ground turkey meat. Then add the onions and the garlic and let them cook for about 5–10 minutes. Next, add the marinara sauce. Stir to mix. Then add the broccoli to the mix and stir again. Let it cook for 5–10 minutes. In a small bowl mix the Chavrie with the egg, stir until well combined. Spray a 9"x13" baking dish with oil. Start with a little sauce in the bottom of the dish. Just barely enough to cover it like the oil. Then start to layer the dish with the uncooked noodles, cheese spread, sauce, shredded or sliced cheddar or mozzarella cheese. Repeat until the baking dish is full. Cover with foil and bake for 1 hour at 350 degrees.

Serves 6–12.

*Tip – Meyenberg Cheddar Goat Cheese shreds easier than Woolwich Cheddar or Mozzarella Goat Cheese. If you are using the Woolwich it might be easier to slice, it very thinly just as the Vegan Gourmet Cheeses.

This recipe contains goat casein which is different from cow casein. Check with your doctor first to see if goat casein is acceptable for you.

Busy Day Burritos (GFCF)

1 pkg. Brown Rice Tortillas Food for Life
1 pkg. Lunch Meat Hormel Natural Choice or Applegate Farms
1 pkg. Cheddar Cheese shredded (Goat or Vegan Gourmet)
Mustard Annie's Naturals optional
Sea Salt optional
Garlic Powder optional
Onion Powder optional

Place a tortilla on a microwave safe plate and spread your favorite mustard on it or sprinkle lightly with Worcestershire sauce. Then place the shredded cheddar cheese onto the tortilla and sprinkle with your favorite spices. Next add the lunch meat on top of the cheese. It can be beef, turkey, ham or chicken whatever you like. Next microwave for 1 minute at 60% power just enough to melt the cheese. Then roll the burritos up and enjoy. It should work with the Vegan Gourmet Cheese to but I have not yet used that one on this recipe. Just watch it in the microwave you may have to adjust the temperature setting. Firm goat cheese works best for shredding like Meyenberg.

This recipe contains goat casein which is different from cow casein. Check with your doctor first to see if goat casein is acceptable for you.

Chicken Pasta Salad (GFCF)

2 c. uncooked Rice Elbow Pasta, cook according to pkg.

2–10 oz. cans White Chicken in Water Valley Fresh drained

½ c. Pickle Relish Bubbies or Cascadian Farm

1–16 oz. pkg. Peas & Carrots frozen, thawed

¾ c. Canola Mayonnaise Spectrum

½ tsp. Onion Powder pure or Onion chopped to taste

½ tsp. Garlic Powder pure or Garlic chopped

½ tsp. Paprika pure

2 lg. Eggs hard-boiled, chopped

½ c. Black Olives sliced Santa Barbara

4–6 slices Bacon cooked, crumbled Beeler's or Applegate Farms

Place all the ingredients into a large container with a lid and stir. Refrigerate for a few hours before serving. Serve on a bed of your favorite salad greens. The salad can be topped with shredded cheddar cheese (GFCF or goat). Sprinkle the top with a little more paprika to garnish. This recipe makes a nice summer dinner.

Serves 3–6.

*This recipe contains goat casein which is different from cow casein. Check with your doctor first to see if goat casein is acceptable for you.

Macaroni & Cheese (GFCF)

2 c. Macaroni uncooked Tinkyada

2 c. Rice Milk Pacific

¾ lb. Cheddar Goat Cheese or Vegan Gourmet shredded

4 Tbsp. Sweet Rice Flour

4 Tbsp. Margarine Earth Balance Stick

1 tsp. Sea Salt

1 tsp. Mustard dry ground

1 tsp. Paprika

Cook the macaroni according to the package directions. Then drain and set aside. In a 2–qt. saucepan melt the margarine, then add the flour to it and stir to make a paste. Next add the milk and the spices. Stir constantly over a low heat until all the lumps are broken up and the sauce is smooth. Reserve a small amount of the shredded cheese to garnish the dish. Start adding part of the shredded cheese to the sauce and continue to stir it while the cheese is melting into the sauce. Repeat that 2 or 3 times until all the cheese is worked into the sauce except the garnish amount. Place half of the macaroni into a margarine coated 7"x11" baking dish. Then pour half of the cheese sauce on top of the macaroni. Repeat with the other half of the macaroni and cheese sauce. Garnish with the reserved shredded cheese and sprinkle with paprika. Bake at 350 degrees for approximately 20 minutes.

This recipe contains goat casein which is different from cow casein. Check with your doctor first to see if goat casein is acceptable for you.

Maple Pork Sausage (GFCF)

1 lb. Ground Pork lean or other ground meat
3 Tbsp. Sweet Rice Flour
½ c. Water
¾ c. Maple Syrup "Grade A" Dark Amber
1 tsp. Sea Salt
1 tsp. Garlic Powder
1 tsp. Onion Powder
½ tsp. Sage – Rubbed
½ tsp. Black Pepper optional

In a 2 c. measuring cup place the sweet rice flour and water, stir it until there are no lumps in it. Add the maple syrup to the measuring cup and stir again. Brown the ground pork well. Drain the meat if necessary. Add the spices to the meat and stir. Add the maple sauce to meat and stir again. Keep stirring until the meat and sauce become thick.

Serves 3.

I use a lodge logic iron skillet. I keep a thin layer of olive oil in it. It is very close to non-stick with out the harmful synthetic materials.

Meat-loaf (GFCF)

1–1¼ lbs. Ground Turkey or Beef

2 lg. Eggs beaten with a fork

¾ c. Bread Crumbs dry Orgran Rice Crumbs

½ c. Rice Milk Pacific

¼ c. Onion chopped or dehydrated, reconstituted and drained

1–4 oz. can Mushrooms, chopped

2 Tbsp. Parsley Flakes dried

½ tsp. Oregano

½ tsp. Sea Salt

½ tsp. Garlic Powder pure

½ tsp. Paprika pure

2 Tbsp. Ketchup Annie's Naturals

2 tsp. Worcestershire Sauce GF

Mix all the ingredients (except the meat) in a large mixing bowl. Then add the meat and stir again. Use a 9" deep-dish pie plate or an oval platter with a raised lip. Place the meat onto the dish and shape it into a ring or oval with a 2–inch diameter hole in the center. Use wax paper to cover the meat. Then, microwave on high for 15 minutes or until no pink remains in the center of the meat. To bake: place the meat into a loaf pan and bake at 350 degrees for 45–50 minutes. The meat-loaf can be topped with Mushroom Onion Sauce or Sweet Black Cherry BBQ Sauce when served.

Serves 3–6.

Mushroom Onion Sauce (GFCF)

1–4.5 oz. jar Mushroom slices, drained
¼ c. Onion chopped or dehydrated, reconstituted and drained
1 Tbsp. Margarine Earth Balance Buttery Sticks
1 Tbsp. Sweet Rice Flour
½ tsp. Sea Salt
1½ Tbsp. Worcestershire Sauce GF
¾ c. Rice Milk Pacific
½ c. Sour Cream Tofutti

Place the mushrooms, onions, and margarine in a 4–cup microwavable bowl. Microwave uncovered on high for 2 minutes. Then add the flour, salt, and the Worcestershire sauce. Stir in all of the milk. Microwave the sauce uncovered 2 to 4 minutes on high, stirring every minute. It should thicken and be bubbly. Next, stir in the sour cream. Microwave approximately 30 seconds more, stirring once. Do not boil it. Serve.

Oven Style Fried Chicken (GFCF)

1–1¼ lbs. Chicken thighs boneless/skinless

1 lg. Egg beaten

½ c. Batter Coating Mix

½ c. Margarine Stick Earth Balance sliced into pats

Break an egg into a small dish that is large, enough to place a chicken thigh. Lightly scramble the egg with a fork. In another small dish that is large, enough to place a chicken thigh put the batter coating mix. Then dip one chicken thigh into the egg first on both sides. Next dip the chicken thigh into the batter coating on both sides. Place in a 9"x 11" baking dish. Repeat for all the remaining pieces of chicken. With the remaining batter coating in the dish, sprinkle it over the top of the coated chicken or throw away. Do not reuse any batter coating that has encountered raw meat. Place sliced margarine pats around the sides of the dish and in between the pieces of meat. Bake at 375 degrees for 55–60 minutes. Do not turn the meat over.

Serves 3 to 6.

Pizza Crust (GFCF)

½ c. Shortening Spectrum melted

1 1/3 c. Sweet Rice Flour

2/3 c. Arrowroot Starch

2 tsp. Sea Salt

1 tsp. Garlic powder pure

1 tsp. Onion powder pure

1 tsp. Oregano dried

1 tsp. Calcium powder Kirkman

½ tsp. Xanthan Gum or Guar Gum

½ c. Rice Milk Pacific

4 lg. Eggs

Measure the shortening first and place it on a low heat to melt it. In a medium mixing bowl place all the dry ingredients and stir lightly to mix. Add the milk and the eggs and stir again. Then add the melted shortening and stir again, until mixed together good. Use a clay baking sheet and spread the dough with a rubber scraper. Next spread with your favorite tomato sauce and add toppings. Bake at 400 degrees for about 25–30 minutes. Lower the rack from the middle position to the lowest or next to the lowest.

Salmon Patties (GFCF)

1 can Salmon meat

1 c. Brown Rice Bread Crumbs Hol-Grain

1 lg. Egg

1 tsp. Sea Salt

¼ tsp. Paprika

Place all the ingredients into a small mixing bowl and stir well.

Form into patties with your hands. Then place into a frying pan with some olive oil and fry on both sides until crisp and done in the center.

Scalloped Potato Casserole (GFCF)

4 lg. Potatoes peeled and sliced

1 lb. Lean Ground Beef browned

½ c. Onion dehydrated and reconstituted or fresh chopped

1 tsp. Garlic chopped or Powder

¼ c. Margarine Earth Balance Buttery Sticks

¼ c. Sweet Rice Flour

2½ c. Rice Milk Pacific

1 tsp. Sea Salt

½ tsp. Paprika

2–15 oz. cans Sweet Peas drained

1 bk. Cheddar Goat Cheese or Cheese Substitute

Brown the meat in a large frying pan with a little olive oil then, add the onions and garlic. Cook until the onions are tender. Next add the drained peas. Stir and remove from the heat. Melt the margarine in a 2–quart saucepan. Then add the sea salt, paprika, and flour. Stir into a paste. Add the milk all at once and stir over medium/low heat continuously to remove any lumps and the sauce becomes thick. Place half of the sliced potatoes into a margarine coated 9"x13" baking dish. Next add the meat mixture and half of the sauce. Make another layer with the remaining potatoes and sauce. Cover and bake at 350 degrees for 35 minutes. Then uncover and top with shredded cheddar goat cheese and sprinkle with paprika. Bake for 30 minutes more. Let stand for approximately 5 minutes then, serve.

Serves 6.

This recipe contains goat casein which is different from cow casein. Check with your doctor first to see if goat casein is acceptable for you.

SIDE
DISHES

Deviled Eggs (SCD)

6 lg. Eggs hard-boiled, shelled
2 tsp. Mustard Annie's Naturals
2 Tbsp. Canola Mayonnaise Spectrum
½ tsp. Sea Salt
Paprika

Cut the eggs in half lengthwise. Remove the yolks and mash them in a small bowl. Then add the other ingredients to the yolks and stir until mixed well. Refill the egg whites with the yolk mixture. The mixture can be placed into a decorators' bag with a large star tip and squeezed back into the whites for a fancy look. Dust with paprika. Refrigerate.

Variations:
1 Tbsp. Pickle Relish
1 Tbsp. crisp Bacon crumbled, garnish with a small piece of bacon
1 tsp. Hot Pepper Sauce   Check Ingredients!

*Tip – The pickle relish variation and the bacon variation will not work with a decorators' bag. The chunks will block the star tip from working.

Fried Mushrooms and Onions (SCD)

1–12 oz. pkg. Mushrooms white button sliced or other
1 medium/large Sweet Onion chopped
1 heaping tsp. Garlic chopped
½ tsp. Sea Salt
Olive Oil

Cover the bottom of a large frying pan with olive oil. Then add the garlic first. Turn heat to medium, when the garlic starts to smell good, usually a few minutes. Then add the mushrooms and onions. Stir well and add more olive oil if needed. Keep stirring uncovered. If the oil starts to pop, cover it with a splatter screen. It fries quicker if you don't cover it right away. Fry until desired crispiness is achieved. We like ours really crisp, almost burnt.

Mashed Sweet Carrots (SCD)

1 lb. Baby Carrots
Clover Honey
Cinnamon ground

Steam the carrots until they are very soft. Puree in a food processor until smooth. Serve onto the plates. Drizzle with honey and sprinkle heavy with cinnamon.

Pickled Eggs & Beets (SCD)

2–15 oz. cans Beets medium whole
2 c. Beet juice approximately from the cans, save
12 lg. Eggs hard-boiled, shelled
½ c. Clover Honey
1 c. Apple Cider Vinegar
½ c. Chopped Onion frozen, thawed
1 tsp. Sea Salt
½ tsp. Cinnamon ground

Hard-boil the eggs. Adding approximately 2 Tbsp. of vinegar to the water will make shelling the eggs easier. Also if you are using a stainless steel pot, it cleans off any hard water marks so you get a two for one deal and a nice clean pot. Cool the eggs by draining them and running cold water over them. When they are cool shell the eggs. Place them in a 12–cup container with a lid. In a 4–cup measuring cup drain the beet juice. Place the whole drained beets in with the eggs and add the chopped onion. Add the sea salt, cinnamon, honey, and the vinegar to the beet juice and stir until the honey is completely dissolved. Then pour the juice mixture over the eggs, beets, and the onions. Stir, then cover and let stand in the refrigerator for 2 days or more. To get the pink color to the edge of the yolks takes about 5 days.

Spinach and Mushrooms (SCD)

2–6 oz. pkgs. Spinach Organic

2 Tbsp. Olive Oil

1 tsp. Garlic chopped Christopher Ranch Organic

1–8 oz. pkg. Mushrooms sliced white button or other

½ tsp. Sea Salt

¼ tsp. Paprika

6 strips Bacon very crisp

If buying spinach by the bunch, wash it first. I'm usually in a hurry so I buy Spinach that is already washed and mushrooms that are already washed and sliced. In a large frying pan, heat the olive oil over medium heat. Add the garlic and sauté until you can smell it but not brown, then add the mushrooms and turn the heat to medium high. Cook stirring until mushrooms become caramelized. Stir in the salt and paprika. Cook until all the moisture has evaporated. Add the spinach to the mushrooms and turn down the heat to medium. Cook and stir just until the spinach wilts. Add the crumbled bacon and serve.

Squash Chips (SCD)

1 Butternut Squash
Olive Oil
Sea Salt

Wash the squash. Next cut the squash into thin slices, the thinner the better for crispness. Place a single layer on clay baking sheets and spray heavily with olive oil, and then sprinkle with sea salt. Bake at 450 degrees for about 10–15 minutes, then turn them over and spray with olive oil and sprinkle with sea salt again. Return them to the oven and bake for 10–15 minutes more until really crisp. They are very close to potato chips.

Steamed Vegetables (SCD)

1 lb. Peas Organic frozen
3 strips Bacon, crisp and crumbled

Place water in the bottom of the steamer. Then place the steamer rack in the bottom over the water. Pour the peas on the rack. Place the crumbled bacon on top of the peas and cover. Turn the heat onto high to get the water to boil. After it starts boiling good, turn the heat down to save energy. Steam the vegetables for about 15–20 minutes until they are tender. These can be varied on busy days, like green beans with almond slivers and broccoli with honey. Then vary the topping on it like sea salt, honey, butter substitute, cinnamon, and lemon juice. Do the more time demanding side dishes on days when the extra time is available.

Baked Beans (SCD/GFCF)

1 lb. Navy Beans soaked, drained, cooked 4 hrs. on high, and rinsed
5 c. Water
½ c. Onion dehydrated Just Onions or fresh chopped
2 tsp. Sea Salt
5 slices Bacon cooked & crumbled
½ c. Clover Honey
½ tsp. Mustard dry ground
½ c. Ketchup
1½ tsp. Paprika
1½ tsp. Garlic Powder
1½ tsp. Ginger ground
¾ c. Sweet Black Cherry BBQ Sauce

Optional GFCF
2 Tbsp. Sweet Rice Flour

Place all the ingredients into a crock-pot and cook for 6 hours more on high. Add more water if needed.

DAIRY
SUBSTITUTES

Butter Substitute (SCD)

¾ c. Coconut Oil refined (room temperature)
¼ c. Safflower, Olive or Peanut Oil
¼ c. Sunflower Oil
½ tsp. Sesame Oil

Place all the ingredients into a mixer and beat on a medium speed just until mixed. Do not over mix. Store the butter in an airtight container with a lid in the refrigerator. It will keep for up to six weeks or so. Not for cooking.

Nut Milk (scd)

1½ c. Almond Slivers heaping
1 tsp. Calcium Powder Kirkman
2 c. Water

Half size
¾ c. Almond Slivers heaping
½ tsp. Calcium Powder Kirkman
1 c. Water

Blanched nuts will make a whiter milk. Blend all the ingredients well with a food processor. Check the capacity on your food processor. Mine is extra large. Use a mesh coffee filter to strain the solids out. Press down well to get all the liquid out. Yield is about 1¼ cups of nut milk for a full recipe. Save the solids to make a leftover pumpkin cake if desired.

Cheese Substitute American (GFCF)

1 1/3 c. Cashews raw, chopped
½ c. Water
½ c. Yeast Flakes Vegetarian KAL Nutritional
1/3 c. Lemon Juice
2 tsp. Tahini
2½ tsp. Sea Salt
1 tsp. Onion Powder
1 tsp. Garlic Powder
1 tsp. Mustard dry ground
1 tsp. Paprika
1 tsp. Calcium Powder Kirkman

Separate
1½ c. Water
4 tsp. Gelatin Unflavored unsweetened

Place all the ingredients (except 1½ c. water and 4 tsp. gelatin) into a food processor and blend until it is smooth. Bring the water with the gelatin to a boil, turn the heat down, and gently boil for 3 minutes, stirring occasionally. Then add to the food processor mix and blend again. Immediately pour into a sprayed pan. Tap out the bubbles. Chill in refrigerator. It will set in about an hour or so. It will slice and melt for cheeseburgers and pizza. Yield is slightly over 3 cups. Use a Rubbermaid rectangle container 3.2 cups or 1.6 pints with a little left over that I put into a snack cup for my husbands lunch.

Use an equal amount of agar powder in place of the gelatin for a stiffer block of cheese but it does not melt as easy as using the gelatin.

I used a 14–cup capacity Cuisinart with this recipe. Check your capacity on your food processor. You might have to cut this recipe in half.

Cheese Substitute Ricotta (GFCF)

1–12 oz. Tofu firm
1 lg. Egg
¼ c. Olive Oil
½ tsp. Sea Salt
½ tsp. Nutmeg ground

Place all the ingredients into a small bowl and whisk until it is smooth. This recipe works great with the broccoli lasagna.

DESSERT

Fruit Juice Gelatin (scd)

1¼ c. Fruit Juice like Grape, pure unsweetened R.W. Knudsen
¼ c. Water
1 Tbsp. Gelatin unflavored, unsweetened
1 c. Clover Honey

Place the juice, water, and honey into a medium saucepan and stir. Lightly sprinkle gelatin evenly over the top. Let it stand 5 minutes. Then heat on low until completely dissolved. Pour into desired mold or container and refrigerate to set the gelatin. After the gelatin is set, cover with plastic wrap or put a lid on it.

Fruit Sorbet (SCD)

2–10 oz. Sweet Cherries frozen, thawed
½ c. Clover Honey
4 tsp. Gelatin unflavored unsweetened
1 c. Water
2 Tbsp. Cover Honey dissolved into Hot Water
1/3 c. Hot Water
2 Tbsp. Vanilla Extract or other extract
3 Tbsp. Lemon Juice

Puree the cherries and ½ c. honey and set aside. In a small saucepan place 1 c. water and sprinkle the gelatin over the top of it evenly. Let it stand for about 5 minutes. Stand it over a pan of simmering water (like a double boiler) and stir it until it is completely dissolved. Remove from the heat. Set it aside to cool some. Add 2 Tbsp. honey dissolved into the 1/3 c. hot water, 2 Tbsp. vanilla, 3 Tbsp. lemon juice to the puree. Mix again. Bring the gelatin to the same temperature as the puree, then pour it into the puree and mix well. Freeze the mixture for about 2 hours until partially frozen, stirring occasionally. Freeze until firm. I used a 14–cup capacity Cuisinart with 3/4 h.p. motor. Check your capacity. You may have to cut this recipe in half.

Nut Crust (SCD)

1½ c. Brazilian Nuts finely chopped or other nuts
½ c. Almond Flour
1/8 tsp. Sea Salt
½ tsp. Cinnamon
1 Tbsp. Clover Honey
2 Tbsp. Coconut Oil
1 tsp. Calcium Powder optional

Place all the ingredients into a food processor and blend well. Press the dough into a 9" pie dish with a rubber scraper. Bake at 325 degrees for 10 minutes. Reshape with a fork. Bake for 5 minutes more. Reshape with a fork if needed. Bake 5 minutes more.

Peanut Butter Fudge (SCD)

1½ c. Coconut Oil (refined–no coconut taste)
2 c. Peanut Butter heaping   Check Ingredients!
2 c. Clover Honey
1 tsp. Sea Salt

Melt the coconut oil over a low heat if it is a solid. Then place all the ingredients in a large mixing bowl and whip on a high speed for 2 minutes. Pour into a sprayed 9"x13" dish. Refrigerate. The fudge sets up in about 3–4 hours. Cut into squares and enjoy.

Pumpkin Pie Filling (SCD)

1–15 oz. can Pumpkin Farmers Market Organic
2 lg. Eggs
1/3 c. Clover Honey
1¼ c. Almond Nut Milk
1/8 tsp. Sea Salt
1 tsp. Vanilla Extract
1 tsp. Cinnamon ground
¼ tsp. Cloves ground
¼ tsp. Nutmeg ground
¼ tsp. Ginger ground
1 tsp. Calcium Powder optional
1 Nut Crust already prepared

In a large bowl place all of the ingredients and mix it together well. Pour into the already prepared nut crust. Bake at 320 degrees for 40 minutes approximately. The pie should be set in the center. Let the pie cool completely on a wire rack before refrigerating.

Apple Crisp (GFCF)

6 Granny Smith Apples peeled, cored, sliced and
soaked in water with a little lemon juice
1½ c. Chestnut Flour or other flour
1½ c. Brown Sugar
1 c. Shortening, Spectrum
Nutmeg ground
1 can Soy Whip Soyatoo optional

In a bowl place the flour, sugar, and the shortening. Mix with a fork until it is a crumbly dough. Grease a 9"x13" baking dish. Drain the water off the apples and place them into the dish. Pinch off dime size (pence) pieces of dough and totally cover the apples. Sprinkle with nutmeg to taste. Bake at 350 degrees for about 30 minutes. Serve onto plates and drizzle with caramel syrup and or spray with soy whip. Store leftovers in the refrigerator.

Other GF flours like rice flour can be used in place of the chestnut flour.

Caramel Syrup (GFCF)

¼ tsp. Baking Soda
1 Tbsp. Water
2 c. Evaporated Goat Milk Meyenberg
1 c. White Sugar
1 Tbsp. Clover Honey
1 tsp. Vanilla Extract

In a 3 or 4–qt. sauce pan wipe the upper edge with a little olive oil to help prevent boil-overs. In a small bowl place the water with the baking soda and stir until dissolved. In the sauce pan add the sugar, evaporated milk, honey, and the vanilla. Cook over medium high heat, stirring constantly until simmering. Remove from the heat and add the baking soda mixture, stirring constantly to keep it from boiling over. Place the saucepan back over medium high heat and continue to stir until large, glassy bubbles form approximately 15–20 minutes. Reduce heat to a medium low setting and continue stirring until it turns into a thickened caramel brown syrup. Pour the syrup into a wide-mouthed glass jar with a lid like an old clean pickle jar. Let it cool completely before placing the lid on. Store the caramel in the refrigerator for up to approximately 1 month. Remove before use and warm the jar in a hot water bath to make the caramel easy to spoon out and serve. This syrup is great with ice cream, almond pound cake, cheesecake, and apple crisp.

This recipe contains goat casein which is different from cow casein. Check with your doctor first to see if goat casein is acceptable for you.

Cheesecake (GFCF)

5–5.3 oz. pkgs. Goat Cheese Chavrie or 3–8 oz. pkgs. Tofutti Cream Cheese
2/3 c. Clover Honey
½ c. Sweet Rice Flour + 2 Tbsp. or (Tofutti use ¼ c. flour)
1 tsp. Vanilla Extract pure
3 lg. Eggs
¼ c. Rice Milk Pacific
2 Graham Style Crust already prepared
1 can Soy Whip Soyatoo optional

Place the cheese, honey, flour, and the vanilla in a large mixing bowl. Use an electric mixer to beat until creamy. Add the eggs and beat on a low speed until just mixed. Add the milk and beat again until just mixed. Pour the batter into a prepared crust dish. Garnish with reserved crumbs (optional). Bake at 375 degrees for 40–50 minutes. Cool the cheesecakes completely on a wire rack then refrigerate. This makes enough batter for 2–8" pie plate cheesecakes. Serve the cheesecake with fruit, chocolate syrup, caramel syrup, and or soy whip.

*This recipe contains goat casein which is different from cow casein. Check with your doctor first to see if goat casein is acceptable for you.

Chocolate Fudge (GFCF)

2 sections Chocolate unsweetened Scharffen Berger
3–1 oz. bars Cocoa Butter Lorann Oils
1½ c. Clover Honey
½ tsp. Sea Salt
1 tsp. Vanilla Extract
¼ c. Chestnut Flour
¾ c. Coconut Oil refined

Place the coconut oil, cocoa butter, and the chocolate into a double boiler. Stir constantly while it is melting. Remove the chocolate from heat and add all the other ingredients. Stir really well to make sure that there are no lumps in it. Pour into a sprayed 7"x11" dish and refrigerate. Cut into squares when the fudge has fully set.

Chocolate Syrup (GFCF)

1 c. Clover Honey
1 c. Cocoa Powder unsweetened
¼ c. Water
1/8 tsp. Sea Salt

Place the water and the honey in a medium saucepan. Cook over medium heat, stirring constantly until dissolved. Just when it starts to boil remove from the heat and turn burner down to low. Add the salt and half of the cocoa powder. Continue stirring and return to the heat for about a minute. Remove from the heat and add the other half of the cocoa powder. Continue stirring and return to the heat for about a minute or two until smooth and dissolved. Remove from the heat and let it cool a little. Store in a glass jar with a lid and refrigerate. To make chocolate milk add 2–3 tablespoons of syrup to milk and stir until dissolved. This syrup is great on ice cream, almond pound cake, cheesecake, and dunk marshmallows in it.

Crispy Treats (GFCF)

1 Marshmallow recipe prepared
7 c. Puffed Rice Cereal plain or chocolate
approximately 1 10 – 11.5 oz. box of cereal

Lift the marshmallow from the mixing bowl and place it into a large clean mixing bowl. Then add the cereal and stir well to mix. Next place the mixture into a margarine coated 9"x13" dish. Smooth flat with a rubber spatula and refrigerate to set. After the treats are set approximately 2 hours, cut into bars. Store the treats in the refrigerator.

Graham Style Crust (GFCF)

½ c. + 1 Tbsp. Margarine melted Earth Balance Buttery Sticks

½ c. White Rice Flour

½ c. Brown Rice Flour

1/3 c. Tapioca Starch

1/3 c. Potato Starch

½ c. Brown Sugar packed or Natural Cane Sugar

½ c. Walnuts finely chopped

2 tsp. Cinnamon

1 tsp. Baking Powder Hain Featherweight

1 tsp. Calcium Powder Kirkman's optional

½ tsp. Xanthan Gum or Guar Gum

½ tsp. Sea Salt

Place the margarine in a small pot and melt over low heat. In a small mixing bowl measure and lightly stir all the dry ingredients together. Next stir in the melted margarine with a fork until it is well combined and crumbly. Then press the dough into the bottom of an 8" pie plate. Reserve a small amount of the mix for a garnish (optional). This makes a great cheesecake crust.

Makes two 8" pie plate crusts.

Maple Syrup Fudge (GFCF)

2 c. Maple Syrup pure
¾ c. Evaporated Goat Milk Meyenberg
1 Tbsp. Brown Rice Syrup Lundberg
1 tsp. Vanilla Extract
¾ c. Walnuts finely chopped optional

In a large heavy bottomed 3 or 4–qt. saucepan place the maple syrup, goat milk, and brown rice syrup. Cook over medium heat stirring constantly until it starts to boil. Clip the candy thermometer to the side of the saucepan. Continue to cook without stirring until it reaches 234 degrees on the candy thermometer. Remove the saucepan from the heat and do not stir. Let the fudge stand until it cools down to about 110 to 120 degrees. Then beat the fudge with a spoon until it thickens and starts to lose its gloss. Next add the vanilla and the walnuts and stir again quickly. Pour quickly into a buttered 7"x9" baking dish and refrigerate. When the fudge is set completely, cut into squares.

This recipe contains goat casein which is different from cow casein. Check with your doctor first to see if goat casein is acceptable for you.

Mellow Fudge (GFCF)

¾ c. Margarine Earth Balance Buttery Sticks

3 c. Natural Sugar

2/3 c. Evaporated Goat Milk Meyenberg

2 c. Semi-sweet Chocolate Chips Tropical Source

1 c. Ricemellow Creme Suzanne's

1 tsp. Vanilla Extract pure

1 c. Nuts chopped (optional)

In a 3–quart saucepan, melt the margarine over medium heat. Next add the sugar and the milk then, stir well. Continue stirring until the mixture boils good for 3 or 4 minutes. Then add in the chocolate chips, ricemellow creme, vanilla, and the nuts if being used. Stir well and pour into a margarine greased 9"x11" baking dish. Refrigerate to cool and then cut into squares.

Microwave Fudge (GFCF)

2–10 oz. bags Chocolate Chips Tropical Source
½ c. Evaporated Goat Milk Meyenberg
½ c. Brown Rice Syrup Lundberg
2 tsp. Vanilla Extract pure
1½ c. Nuts finely chopped optional

Goat butter or margarine coat a 7"x11" baking dish. In a 2–qt. microwavable bowl place the chocolate chips, goat milk, and the brown rice syrup. Stir to mix then, microwave on high for 1 minute. Stir again to mix well and microwave on high for 1 minute again. Add the vanilla and the nuts and stir well to mix then, pour the fudge into the prepared baking dish. Refrigerate the fudge and when it is set (firm), cut into squares. Check your microwave's wattage; more time may need to be added to get the chocolate chips to melt completely. It should be smooth.

This recipe contains goat casein which is different from cow casein. Check with your doctor first to see if goat casein is acceptable for you.

Orange Marshmallow Dessert (GFCF)

2 c. Water boiling
1–3 oz. Orange Jel Dessert Mix
1 c. Ricemellow Creme Suzanne's
1¼ c. Marshmallows mini or large cut into pieces Elyon or Manischewitz
Chocolate Sprinkles Miss Roben's optional
Orange segments or slices optional

Place the marshmallows in the bottom of sundae glasses. Dissolve the jel with boiling water and whisk. Then quickly add the marshmallow creme and whisk again. Quickly pour the jel into the sundae glasses with the marshmallows. Garnish with the chocolate sprinkles and refrigerate. Optional garnish with the orange segments or slices only right before serving.

Serves 6.

FUN
STUFF

Gummi Candy (SCD)

1½ c. Fruit Juice pure unsweetened R.W. Knudsen
1 c. Clover Honey
½ c. Water
18 tsp. Gelatin unsweetened unflavored

Place the juice, water, and the honey into a medium saucepan and stir. Lightly sprinkle the gelatin evenly over the top of the liquid in the saucepan and let it stand 5 minutes. Then heat the saucepan on low until completely dissolved. Pour the candy into small chocolate molds that have been sprayed with olive oil. Place in the freezer for 5 minutes; when set, unmold. I live in a hot climate so I stored mine in an airtight container with wax paper between the layers in the refrigerator.

Hard Candy (scd)

2 c. Clover Honey or billybee Spreadable Honey
1 tsp. Apple Cider Vinegar
1 dram Lorann Oils Natural and Pure Only

Don't try to make this on a humid day. It works best on a dry day. Hard candy molds are WHITE plastic not clear. Lightly spray the candy molds with olive oil to make unmolding easier and place sticks in for lollipops. Place the 4–cup glass measuring cup in a hot water bath to warm the glass up. Due to the very high temperature of this candy a wooden spoon works well. When the candy is close to 290 degrees remove the measuring cup from the hot water bath and dry it completely. Then lightly spray the inside of it with olive oil. This will help to keep the candy from sticking to the inside of the measuring cup as the candy starts cooling off quickly. In a 3 or 4–qt. heavy bottomed saucepan or dutch oven wipe the top edge of the saucepan with olive oil this helps prevent boil overs. Put the honey and the vinegar in the saucepan and stir to mix it until the honey is dissolved. Stir until it comes to a boil. Clip the candy thermometer on the side of the saucepan. Heat on medium heat until it reaches 310 degrees (hard crack). Remove from heat and add the flavoring oil, stir quickly to mix it. Quickly pour it into the warmed glass measuring cup. Then quickly pour it into individual molds before the candy hardens into the measuring cup. Run hot water into the saucepan and the measuring cup to melt off any remaining candy that hardened on it. Let the candy cool completely then unmold and wrap into plastic wrappers.

Hard candy molds are WHITE plastic. Chocolate molds are clear plastic. Candy molds, sticks, wrappers and oils can be found at Cake and Candy Supply Stores or Michael's has a small selection. Lorann Oils that are Natural and Pure Flavors that I have found are: Sassafras, Spearmint, Peppermint, Lime, Orange, Lemon, and Tangerine. Extracts with alcohol tend to burn off at high temperatures so there is not much flavor when finished. When making more than one flavor use tiny colored dot sticker from an office supply store on the wrapper for the different flavors like lemon-yellow, lime-green, etc... The easiest mold to unmold that I have found is Country Kitchen 1½" wide flat round lollipop mold.

Matthew's E-Z Lemonade (SCD)

1 c. Clover Honey
1 c. Water
2 c. Lemon Juice Santa Cruz or fresh squeezed
4 c. Water

Lightly spray the measuring cup with olive oil so the honey will pour quickly. In a 2–quart pitcher with a lid, add the 1 c. of water with the honey. Then, cap and shake the pitcher until the honey is completely dissolved. Next add the lemon juice and the remaining water to make 2 quarts, shake again. Refrigerate and shake well before serving.

Party Punch (SCD)

1 c. Clover Honey

1 c. Water

2 c. Black Cherry Juice unsweetened R.W. Knudsen

2 c. Concord Grape Juice unsweetened

2 c. Pineapple Juice unsweetened

Lightly spray the measuring cup with olive oil so the honey will pour quickly. In a 2–quart pitcher with a lid, add the 1 c. of water with the honey. Then, cap and shake the pitcher until the honey is completely dissolved. Then add the juices or you will end up with about 2" of foam on the top of the container. This recipe makes 2 quarts of punch. Float lemon, lime, and orange slices for a garnish. If a sparkling punch is desired, use some carbonated water or Dr. Tima Natural Ginger Ale after the original mix is done.

Tart Citrus Punch (SCD)

½ c. Clover Honey

½ c. Cold Water

3 c. Orange Juice pure unsweetened

2 c. Pineapple Juice pure unsweetened

2 c. Lime Juice pure unsweetened

Lightly spray the measuring cup with olive oil so the honey will pour quickly. In a 2–quart pitcher with a lid, add the ½ c. of water with the honey. Then, cap and shake the pitcher until the honey is completely dissolved. Next add the lime, pineapple, and orange juices. Shake again and refrigerate to chill. Pour into a punch bowl and garnish with thin orange or lime slices optional.

Tina's Turkey Jerky (SCD)

3 lbs. Ground Turkey Meat 85% Lean works the best
1/3 c. Water
2 tsp. Garlic Powder
2 tsp. Onion Power
2 tsp. Sage
2 tsp. Ginger ground
1 tsp. Sea Salt

Blend all the ingredients in a large bowl. We use a Nesco American Harvest dehydrator with 7 trays and the jerky press. Fill the press with the meat mixture. Squeeze the strips onto the trays. Sprinkle the tops of the strips good with sea salt. In our dry climate, it's done in about 12 hours. It is great for hiking and quick, traveling lunches.

Turkey Jerky (SCD)

3 lbs. Ground Turkey Meat 85% Lean works the best
1/3 c. Water
3 Tbsp. Spice blend Nantucket Off-Shore Mt. Olympus
1 tsp. Sea Salt
3/4 tsp. Garlic Powder
3/4 tsp. Onion Power

Blend all the ingredients in a large bowl. We use a Nesco American Harvest dehydrator with 7 trays and the jerky press. Fill the press with the meat mixture. Squeeze the strips onto the trays. Sprinkle the tops of the strips good with sea salt. In our dry climate it's done in about 12 hours. It is great for hiking and quick, traveling lunches. Other favorites are Prairie Rub, Renaissance Rub, and Holiday Turkey Rub.

Cinnamon Nut Candy (SCD/GFCF)

½ c. Cinnamon Honey Crème Honey Acres

½ c. Natural Peanut Butter creamy

1½ tsp. Cinnamon ground

¼ c. Almond Flour or Hazelnut Flour

½ c. Cashews roasted and salted, finely chopped

Optional GFCF

¼ c. Chestnut Flour

In a small bowl, stir the cinnamon honey crème, peanut butter, and cinnamon together. A small amount of olive oil on your hands will help to keep the candy from sticking to them. Then add the almond flour and knead it in. Roll the candy into bite size balls. Place the chopped cashews into a small bowl. Place a small ball into the cashews and cover the top of it. Smash the ball with your thumb into a disk. Store the candy in an airtight container with a lid.

*I recently found another honey called billybee Spreadable Honey. It seems to be about the same consistency and should also work for this recipe. Just increase the amount of cinnamon to 2 tsp.

Colored Eggs (SCD/GFCF)

White Eggs
4–6 or more Onion Skins (Different kinds give you slightly different colors
from a deep reddish/purple to a lighter reddish/brown.)
3 tsp. White Vinegar
1 tsp. Salt

In a large saucepan place the onion skins on the bottom. Place the eggs in, and then fill with water until the eggs are covered about 1½–2 inches from the top of pot. Add the salt and the vinegar. Boil like regular hard-boiled eggs, gently stirring occasionally. It will stain plastic spoons. Try not to scrape the eggs with the spoon or it might leave a white scratch mark. Drain and blot dry with a paper towels.

Marshmallows (SCD/GFCF)

1 c. Clover Honey
½ c. Boiling Water
6 tsp. Gelatin unflavored, unsweetened
2 tsp. Vanilla Extract or other extract
1 c. Cashews chopped optional
Coconut Flour or Dry Roasted Hazelnut Flour optional

Optional GFCF
Tapioca Starch or Potato Starch

Spray a 9"x13" dish with olive oil. In a large mixing bowl dissolve the gelatin in the boiling water. Add the honey and the extract. Whip on high until very thick with stiff peaks. If using cashews add them now and stir with a spoon. Pour into the dish and chill for at least 2 hours. Cut into squares with a wet knife. Roll in coconut flour or dry roasted hazelnut flour. Store the marshmallows in an airtight container in the refrigerator. The marshmallows last about two weeks in the refrigerator.

For variety, change the extract to peppermint, cinnamon, almond, orange, etc…

Barbecue Dip (GFCF)

1–8 oz. pkg. Cream Cheese Tofutti or 2–5.3 oz. Chavrie Goat Cheese
½ c. Sweet Black Cherry BBQ Sauce
2 Tbsp. Chives, chopped
2 Tbsp. Parsley Flakes

In a small bowl whisk together all the ingredients until well blended. Cover with a lid and store in the refrigerator. Serve with chips, crackers, and or vegetables.

This recipe contains goat casein which is different from cow casein. Check with your doctor first to see if goat casein is acceptable for you.

Candied Party Nuts (GFCF)

½ c. White Sugar

½ c. Water

½ tsp. Cinnamon ground

½ tsp. Nutmeg ground

½ tsp. Sea Salt optional

1 c. Almonds

1½ c. Cashews roasted

1 c. Walnuts

In a large heavy bottomed saucepan add the sugar, water, cinnamon, nutmeg and the salt together stirring constantly. Bring it to a boil over medium heat and continue to boil, constantly stirring until it is reduced to approximately 1/3 cup and is starting to jel. Quickly add all the nuts and stir until the nuts are all coated. Then spread the nuts onto a foil lined baking sheet. Break up the large clumps of nuts with the spoon. Let the nuts cool completely then break apart into individual nuts. Store the nuts in an air tight container at room temperature for approximately one month.

Caramel Candies (GFCF)

1 c. Goat Butter Meyenberg
2¼ c. Brown Sugar packed or 16 oz.
1¼ c. Evaporated Goat Milk 14 oz. Meyenberg
1 c. Brown Rice Syrup Lundberg
1 tsp. Vanilla Extract pure

Use a 7"x11" baking dish and line it completely with foil. Goat butter the bottom and the sides of the foil. Use a dutch oven or a very large pot. Wipe the edge of the pot with olive oil to help prevent boil-over. Melt the goat butter over a low heat. Then add the evaporated goat milk, brown sugar, and the brown rice syrup, stir well. Turn the heat to a medium/high setting. Cook and stir to boiling. Clip a candy thermometer to the side of the pan. Turn the heat down to a medium setting. Cook and stir until it reaches 248 degrees or a firm-ball stage approximately 30 minutes. Remove from heat and remove the thermometer. Add the vanilla and stir it in quickly. Quickly pour the caramel into the foil lined baking dish. Cool completely or if in a hot climate refrigerate. Take a goat buttered knife and cut into small squares. The caramels can be wrapped individually with plastic wrap. The caramels have been tasted by people not on special diets and they have said it was the best caramels they have ever had.

This recipe contains goat casein which is different from cow casein. Check with your doctor first to see if goat casein is acceptable for you.

Chocolate Covered Eggs (GFCF)

1½ c. Tapioca Starch
1½ c. Powdered Sugar Miss Roben's corn-free
¾ c. Margarine Earth Balance Buttery Sticks
¾ c. Ricemellow Crème Suzanne's
½ c. Sunflower Seed Butter Natural Sunbutter
1 tsp. Vanilla Extract pure
½ tsp. Calcium Powder Kirkman
2–10 oz. bags Chocolate Chips Tropical Source

Cream the margarine and the sugar together in a large mixing bowl. Then, add the ricemellow creme, vanilla, and the sunbutter to the mixture, combine well. Next add the tapioca starch and the calcium powder together in a small bowl and lightly stir well before adding it to the creamed mixture. Use approximately 1/3 of a cup to form egg shapes with your hands and set on wax paper. Use a double boiler or the microwave to melt the chocolate chips. When all the chips have melted and the chocolate is smooth, use a large serving spoon to dip the eggs into the chocolate. Then return the eggs to the wax paper to set, until the chocolate is firm. In hot climates refrigerate. Decorate with royal icing in a decorator's bag optional.

Makes approximately 9 large 2 serving eggs.

Chocolate Covered Marshmallows (GFCF)

1–2 bags 10 oz. Chocolate Chips Tropical Source
1–2 bags 7 oz. Marshmallows large Elyon or Manischewitz

Using a double boiler melt, the chocolate chips until smooth. Using a toothpick in the end of the marshmallow, dip it into the melted chocolate until completely covered. Place the coated marshmallow on wax paper to cool until set or refrigerate for hot climates. Repeat until the desired amount is reached. Decorate with royal icing in a decorator's bag optional.

Easy Peanut Brittle (GFCF)

1 c. Sugar

½ c. Brown Rice Syrup Lundberg

1 c. Spanish Peanuts raw

1 Tbsp. Molasses unsulphured

1 Tbsp. Margarine Earth Balance Buttery Sticks

1 tsp. Vanilla Extract pure

¾ tsp. Baking Soda

Check your microwave's power compared to mine listed on the equipment page. The temperature setting might have to be slightly adjusted for differences. In an 8–cup glass measuring cup like Pyrex place a little olive oil on a paper towel and wipe the first 1" next to the rim to help prevent boil-overs. Then place the peanuts, sugar, brown rice syrup, and the molasses in the measuring cup and stir to mix. Next microwave the candy at 75% power for 4 minutes. Remove and stir with a wooden spoon. Then microwave at 75% power for 4 more minutes. Next add the vanilla and the margarine and quickly stir again. Then place in the microwave for 1 minute at 100% power. Remove and quickly add the baking soda and stir well. Pour/scoop onto a foil lined small baking sheet and spread quickly with the spoon. This will start to set fast. Run hot water over the measuring cup and spoon to melt off any that has hardened onto them. When the candy is cool break it into bite size pieces.

Hard Candy (GFCF) Corn-free

3¾ c. White Sugar
1½ c. Brown Rice Syrup Lundberg
1 c. Water
1 dram Lorann flavoring oil pure

Don't try to make this on a humid day. It works best on a dry day. Hard candy molds are WHITE plastic not clear. Lightly spray the candy molds with olive oil to make unmolding easier and place sticks in for lollipops. Place the 4–cup glass measuring cup in a hot water bath to warm the glass up. Due to the very high temperature of this candy a wooden spoon works well. When the candy is close to 290 degrees remove the measuring cup from the hot water bath and dry it completely. Then lightly spray the inside of it with olive oil. This will help to keep the candy from sticking to the inside of the measuring cup as the candy starts cooling off quickly. In a 3 or 4–qt. heavy bottomed saucepan or dutch oven wipe the top edge of the saucepan with olive oil this helps prevent boil overs. Then place the sugar, brown rice syrup, and water into the saucepan. Stir over medium heat until the sugar is dissolved. Clip the candy thermometer on the saucepan. Boil without stirring until the temperature reaches 310 degrees or hard crack. Remove from heat and quickly stir in the flavoring oil well. Pour the liquid candy into the warmed glass measuring cup. Then quickly pour it into individual molds before the candy hardens in the measuring cup. Run hot water into the saucepan and the measuring cup to melt off any remaining candy that hardened on it. Let the candy cool completely then unmold and wrap in plastic wrappers.

Hard candy molds are WHITE plastic. Chocolate molds are clear plastic. Candy molds, sticks, wrappers and oils can be found at Cake and Candy Supply Stores or Michael's has a small selection. Lorann Oils that are Natural and Pure Flavors that I have found are: Sassafras, Spearmint, Peppermint, Lime, Orange, Lemon, and Tangerine. Extracts with alcohol tend to burn off at high temperatures so there is not much flavor when finished. When making more than one flavor use tiny colored dot stickers from an office supply store on the wrapper for the different flavors like lemon-yellow, lime-green, etc... The easiest mold to unmold that I have found is Country Kitchen 1½" wide flat round lollipop mold.

Hard Set Play Dough (GFCF)

2 c. Salt
2/3 c. Water
1 c. Cornstarch
½ c. Cold Water

Place the salt and the 2/3 c. water in a medium saucepan. Cook over low heat. Heat until it becomes bubbly. Remove from heat and add the cornstarch dissolved in the ½ c. cold water. Stir quickly, mix with hands if necessary. We used latex kitchen gloves to mix it. If the dough is too dry, add a little water to it. Hardens at room temperature in about 36 hours and can be painted with poster type paint. This recipe is great for handprints or science projects. If there are leftovers, wrap it tight in plastic wrap and refrigerate.

I have not yet tried this with potato, arrow root, or tapioca starch for those who are highly allergic to corn but in theory it should work with that too.

Non Dairy Dip (GFCF)

1–8 oz. Cream Cheese Tofutti or 2–5.3 oz. pkgs. Chavrie Goat Cheese
½ c. Sour Cream Tofutti
¼ c. Honey Spreadable billybee
¼ c. Maple Syrup pure or Maple Butter non dairy pure
¼ tsp. Xanthan Gum or Guar Gum

In a small mixing bowl whisk together all the ingredients until well blended. Place in a small container with a lid and refrigerate until needed. Serve with chips, crackers, vegetables, and or fruit.

*This recipe contains goat casein which is different from cow casein. Check with your doctor first to see if goat casein is acceptable for you.

Onion Dip (GFCF)

1–12 oz. Sour Cream Tofutti
1½ Tbsp. Chives freeze-dried chopped or fresh
¾ tsp. Sea Salt
¾ tsp. Onion Powder pure

In a small mixing bowl whisk together all the ingredients until well blended. Place in a small container with a lid and refrigerate until needed. Serve with chips, crackers, and or vegetables.

Party Mints (GFCF)

2 Tbsp. Margarine Earth Balance Stick or Goat Butter Meyenberg
2 Tbsp. Shortening Spectrum
6 Tbsp. Warm Water
6 c.+ Powdered Sugar 24 oz. + some
½ tsp. Peppermint Oil Lorann

In a large mixing bowl, cream the margarine, shortening, 3 Tbsp. warm water, and 3 c. powdered sugar together well. Then add the remaining 3 Tbsp. warm water, 3 c. powdered sugar, and the peppermint oil. Beat well again. It should be dough like but not too stiff. Spoon onto wax paper that is taped down to the counter and knead. If it is too sticky to knead add a little more powdered sugar and work it in with your hands until it becomes a smooth ball. Then divide the dough in half, covering the half that you are not working with so it won't dry out. Roll out the other half of the dough between two pieces of wax paper to 1/8" thickness. Then use a small cookie cutter to cut the mints. Place them on baking sheets lined with wax paper or parchment paper. Reroll the scraps and repeat. If the dough is a little too dry moisten with a little water. If desired use the royal icing recipe to place a flower or a star on the mints. Let the mints dry completely usually overnight before storing in an air tight container. Place parchment paper or wax paper in between the layers in the container.

*This recipe contains goat casein which is different from cow casein. Check with your doctor first to see if goat casein is acceptable for you.

Party Mix (GFCF)

½ c. Margarine GFCF stick Willow Run

1/3 c. Worcestershire Sauce GFCF

1 tsp. Garlic Powder

1 tsp. Onion Powder

1 tsp. Sea Salt

3 c. Pretzels Glutino

2 c. Cashews roasted

4 c. Corn Crunch-Ems Cereal

4 c. Rice Crunch-Ems Cereal

2 c. Terra Stix

Melt the margarine in a 10"x15" baking dish in the oven at 250 degrees. When the margarine is melted add the Worcestershire sauce, garlic, onion, and the sea salt. Stir it to mix it well. Add all the remaining ingredients and stir well again. Bake at 250 degrees for 1½ hours stirring well every 15 minutes. Cool. Store the party mix in an airtight container. It is a great snack for traveling and hiking.

I have replaced the Terra Frites Seasoned Salt Flavor with Terra Stix due to the fact that I don't believe they make the Frites anymore. If this is not suitable add 2 c. of your favorite nuts, raisins, or roasted pumpkin seeds to this mix.

Soft Play Dough (GFCF)

½ c. Rice Flour or other GF Flour   (Pea Flour – Green)
2 Tbsp. Salt   (Soy Flour – Lt. Yellow)
1 tsp. Cream of Tartar
1/3 c. Water
1 tsp. Cooking Oil
Food Coloring Optional

Measure the flour, salt, and the tartar into a bowl. Boil the water in a saucepan. Pour the boiling water into the flour mixture. Then add the oil to the mixture. Color the dough with food coloring if desired. Stir until mixed, the dough will be sticky. Roll and squeeze the warm dough in hands for at least 5 minutes. The longer it is handled the nicer it gets. Model and explore as with any play dough. Store the play dough in an airtight container or plastic wrap.

RESOURCES

Autism sites

Autism Information at www.autismresearchinstitute.com/
Autism Information at www.autism.org
Autism Information at www.autisminfo.com
In Your Pocket: weighted vests at www.weightedvest.com
Sissel Sit-Fit Cushion at www.sissel-online.com
Manners for the Real World video www.coultervideo.com
A very good source of information on what's in your food (what the long chemical names are) is A Consumer's Dictionary Of Food Additives by Ruth Winter, M.S.
Medic Alert Bracelet www.medicalert.org (Alerts First Responders to GFCF diet)
Mercury Levels in Commercial Fish and Shellfish at www.cfsan.fda.gov
PCA-Rx oral chelation/heavy metal detox at www.maxamlabs.com
Auditory Intervention Training at www.drguyberard.com
Rhythmic Entrainment Intervention at www.reiinstitute.com

SCD sites

www.digestivewellness.com for scd foods
www.HouseOfDavid.net for snack bars
www.honeyacres.com for honey crème, honey pouches
www.breakingtheviciouscycle.com for scd information
www.kirkmanlabs.com for Super Nu-Thera multivitamin, Pro-EFA, calcium powder, TMG, and others
www.aa-foods.com for dehydrated traveling foods
www.larabar.com for snack bars

GFCF sites

www.vancesfoods.com for dairy-free milk mix
www.allergygrocer.com for mixes and corn-free powdered sugar
www.joysoy.com for cheese sauce mix
www.glutenfree.com for mixes, sweet rice flour, and salad dressing packets
www.glutensolutions.com for mixes
www.veganstore.com for CHOCOLATE Dairy Free
www.spoon.com for fruit butters, almond nougats

www.ener-g.com for pretzels, mixes, bread

www.kinnikinnick.com for bread, cookies, Doughnuts !!!

www.glutino.com for big bag pretzels, cookies

www.amys.com for soup, marinara sauce, frozen foods

www.manischewitz.com Manischewitz will send you a list of their products that are GF/CF if you ask.

www.gfcfdiet.com for diet and shopping guide

www.gluten-free.net print the catalog & hi-light the ones you want. With one ream of paper you can print this and the diet above.

www.choclat.com the road to decadence

www.bobsredmill.com for flours-in-bulk

www.countrykitchensa.com for candy making supplies

www.AutismNDI.com for Snack bars

www.indiatree.com for natural food colors and decorations

www.anniesnaturals.com for salad dressing and condiments

www.auntcandice.com for snack bars and mixes

www.abeka.org for homeschool curricula

www.timberdoodle.com for educational tools/supplies and toys

www.meyenberg.com for goat milk products

www.goatmilkicecream.com for Laloo's goat milk ice cream (store locator)

www.minimus.biz for individual packet servings (peanut butter, etc.)

www.tenderizemeat.com for natural meat tenderizer

www.fabesnatural.com for apple and pumpkin pies

For people in Tucson, AZ: New Life Food Store on Broadway. The Wild Oats Store. Educational tools/supplies at Teacher Parent Connection www.teacherparent.com. Tucson Alliance for Autism on Country Club Road (520) 319-5857

For people in Fayetteville NC: Applecrate on Camden Road and on Raeford Road. Educational tools/supplies at School Tools www.schooltoolsabc.com. Fayetteville TEACCH on Stamper Road (919) 437-2517.

TRAVELING TIPS

IF YOU CAN afford it, hotel rooms with microwaves and refrigerators are nice. Continental breakfasts normally offer fruit, but little else for special diets. Igloo makes a large 12-volt/110-volt heater/refrigerator that can be carried from your vehicle to hotel room and back again. Hard-boiled eggs and muffins made in advance make for a nice breakfast. Turkey Jerky and Party Mix made in advance with baby carrots and an organic juice box for lunch. Crackers with peanut butter or cheese are a good lunch too. Then, an Alpine Aire Mountain Chili with a salad for supper with cookies for dessert. You get the idea. Rubbermaid bins are handy for storing and moving special foodstuffs while traveling. We keep one stocked with emergency supplies under the seat in our van. We keep another bin in the closet; it contains more traveling foods and an electric kettle to heat water for dehydrated foods. Keeping everything packed ahead of time allows for "spur-of-the-moment" adventures. Single-serving pouches are great for traveling: Alpine Aire, Honey Acres and Annie's Naturals have pouches of peanut butter, honey and salad dressing respectively that lend themselves to packing ahead of time. When flying for travel place all your food into one carry-on bag. Always pack more food than you think you're going to eat. I try to pack at least an extra two days worth of food and vitamins whenever we go somewhere. PACK the ELECTRIC KETTLE on TOP so right BEFORE the bag goes through x-ray take it out and send it through by itself. This saves time and having strange people pawing through the food you have to eat!

Flying Fish Stew (SCD)

2 envelopes Tomato Powder pure Alpine Aire
1 envelope Green Bean Almondine Alpine Aire
1 envelope Vegetable Mix pure Alpine Aire
1½ c. Albacore Tuna cooked, freeze dried Alpine Aire
5 c. Boiling Water
3–1.25 oz. pouches Honey Hi-Honey Honey Acres optional
½ tsp. Sea Salt approximately optional
½ tsp. Garlic Powder approximately optional
½ tsp. Paprika approximately optional

Alpine Aire Albacore Tuna comes in a 5 oz. can not an envelope. Measure the tuna and the spices and place them in one of the other envelopes or in the container that with be used for mixing. Zip the bag closed tight and place inside another zip close storage bag to prevent leaking. Not for international flights. All envelopes must remain sealed for customs. Using a 3–quart plastic container with a lid, empty all the envelopes except the honey pouches into the container and remove the oxygen absorbers and lightly stir. Then pour in the boiling water and stir again. Cover the container with the lid and wait 15 minutes. Uncover and stir again before serving. Drizzle the honey on after serving onto plates or bowls.

Serves 3–4.

Hotel Room Ketchup (SCD)

In a small bowl place about half of an envelope of Tomato Powder Alpine Aire. Add a small amount of boiling water and stir to make a paste. Then add one pouch of Hi-Honey Honey Acres to the paste and stir. Season with Salt, Garlic, and Onion Powder and stir again.

Makes 3 average servings of ketchup.

Traveling Turkey (SCD/GFCF)

2 envelopes Peaches dehydrated Alpine Aire
2 envelopes Turkey dehydrated Alpine Aire
2 envelopes Peas dehydrated Alpine Aire
5 cups Boiling Water (3 c. Water for No Rice)
3–1.25 oz. pouches Hi-Honey Honey Acres
½ tsp. Sea Salt optional if using Bouillon
½ tsp. Paprika optional if using Bouillon
½ tsp. Garlic Powder optional if using Bouillon
½ tsp. Onion Powder optional if using Bouillon
½ tsp. Oregano dried optional if using Bouillon

Optional GFCF
2 envelopes Rice instant dehydrated Alpine Aire
2 cubes Vegan Vegetable Bouillon with Sea Salt Rapunzel
1 Tbsp. Sweet Rice Flour

Crush the peaches up while they are still in their envelopes. Using a 3–quart plastic container with a lid, empty all the envelopes into the container and remove the oxygen absorbers. Add the bouillon cubes and the sweet rice flour, and stir lightly. Next, pour in the boiling water and stir. Cover and wait for 12 minutes. Uncover and stir again before serving. Drizzle the honey on after serving onto plates. If traveling by plane open one of the envelopes and add spices, bouillon, and flour to it before leaving. Zip the bag closed tight and place inside another zip close storage bag to prevent leaking. Not for international flights. All envelopes must remain sealed for customs.

Serves 3–4.

Hotel Chicken & Rice (GFCF)

2 envelopes Vegetable Mix dehydrated Alpine Aire

2 envelopes Chicken dehydrated Alpine Aire

2 envelopes Brown Rice Instant dehydrated Alpine Aire

2 pkgs. Golden Gravy Mix Road's End Organics

2 cubes Vegan Vegetable Bouillon with Sea Salt Rapunzel

½ tsp. Garlic Powder pure optional

½ tsp. Onion Powder pure optional

½ tsp. Sea Salt optional

5 c. Boiling Water

Place all the dry ingredients into a 3–quart plastic container with a lid. Remove all the oxygen absorbers and stir lightly. Add the boiling water and stir again. Cover with the lid and wait for 15 minutes. Stir again and serve.

Serves 3–4.

Vacation Shepherd's Pie (GFCF)

2 c. Beef dehydrated Alpine Aire

2 c. Peas dehydrated Alpine Aire

¼ c. Onion dehydrated Just Onions

Garlic dehydrated a few pieces to taste

2 pkg. Savory Herb Gravy Mix Road's End Organics

½ tsp. Sea Salt approximately

½ tsp. Worcestershire Sauce or Pepper approximately

4 c. Boiling Water

2¼ c. Potato Flakes or 2 envelopes Alpine Aire

3½ c. Boiling Water

Place the first set of ingredients into a glass pan 7"x11" or plastic container with a lid. Add 4 c. boiling water and stir, then cover and wait 10 minutes. In a separate container or envelope add the boiling water to the potato flakes stir, seal and wait 12–15 minutes. Then stir the first mixture. Stir the potatoes and spread them over the first mixture. If available microwave for 5 minutes on high to keep it hot. Optional sprinkle the top of the potatoes with shredded Goat Cheese or your favorite GF/CF Cheese like Vegan Gourmet.

Serves 4–6.

This recipe contains goat casein which is different from cow casein. Check with your doctor first to see if goat casein is acceptable for you.

CONVERSION
CHARTS

Gas Mark	°C	°F
1	140	284
2	150	302
3	170	338
4	180	356
5	190	374
6	200	392
7	220	428
8	230	446
9	240	464

Imperial (floz)	Metric (ml)	US Cups
1	33	
2	66	1/4
3	99	
4	132	1/2
5	165	
6	198	3/4
7	231	
8	264	1
9	297	
10	330	1 1/4
11	363	
12	396	1 1/2
13	429	
14	462	1 3/4
15	495	
16	528	2

Metric (mm)	Inches
3	1/8
6.25	1/4
12.5	1/2
25	1
50	2
75	3
100	4
150	6
200	8
250	10
300	12

INDEX

W

ISBN.141208355-9

9 781412 083553